M000083600

A Pride
of
Bastards

By the same author

THE HOLLOW CROWNS
A History of the Battles of the Wars of the Roses

THE DECEIVERS
The Solution to the Murder of the Princes in the Tower

THE LORDLY ONES
A History of the Neville Family and their part in the Wars of the Roses

THE POPINJAYS
A History of the Woodville Family and their involvement in
English History during the Late Medieval Age.

A Pride
of
Bastards

A History of the Beaufort family, their origins, and their part in the Agincourt War and the Wars of the Roses.

GEOFFREY RICHARDSON

This edition published 2002

by Baildon Books
P.O. Box 107, SHIPLEY, W. Yorks BD17 6UR

Copyright © 2002 Geoffrey Richardson

All rights reserved. No part of this publication may be
reproduced, stored in a retrieval system, or transmitted
in any form or by any means, electronic, mechanical,
photocopying, recording, or otherwise, without the prior
permission of the publishers.

Printed in Great Britain by
Pennine Printing Services Ltd.
Ripponden, West Yorkshire, England

ISBN 09527621 4 5

*This is my last book and it is appropriate,
nay, essential, that I dedicate it therefore, as I
have done the four preceding works, to my beloved
wife Betty, with whom I trust I shall be
reunited ere long.
"Sleep after toil, port after stormy seas,
Ease after war, death after life
does greatly please."*

CONTENTS

Battlemaps & Illustrations

Houses of York & Beaufort

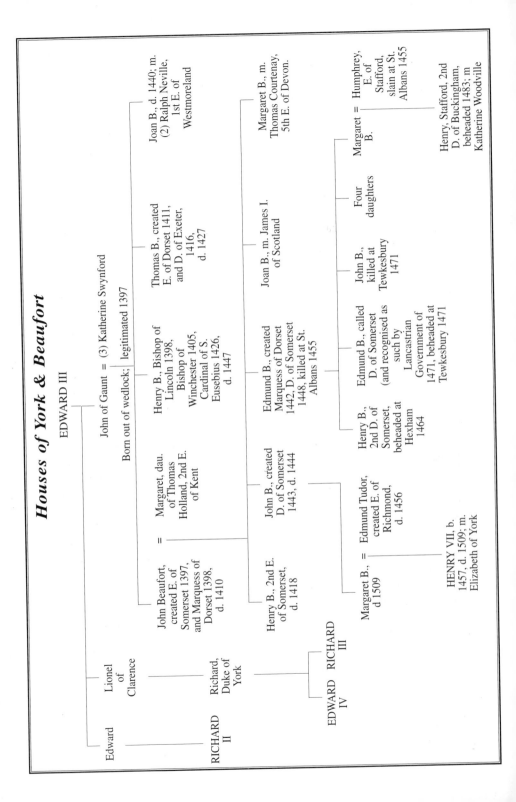

Preface

Six years ago, I began to write a military history of the Wars of the Roses. This was a period in English history which had always fascinated me and, newly retired and needing something to occupy my mind, on a morning in the late winter of 1994/95, I sat down at my dining table [still my work bench today] and started to write my account of First St Albans on a newly acquired word processor.

I had thought that my task would be relatively simple, once I had worked out a basic plot-plan to which I intended to adhere throughout the book. I would begin at the beginning – St Albans – and then carry on through Blore Heath, Northampton, Wakefield and the rest, to the end at Bosworth. However, it quickly became apparent that the task I had set myself was rather more complex than I had imagined. There was a four-year gap between First St Albans and Blore Heath – a period of considerable political change, which had to be covered if the narrative were to make sense. So I realised I would have to write what I came to think of as "inter-chapters", between the accounts of individual battles to provide continuity and from this, it was but a short step to the realisation that a prologue, summarising the causes for the Wars, would be vital for any reader knowing little or nothing of the reasons York and Lancaster had fought for 30 years.

My undertaking was rapidly becoming more complex than I had first thought, but it was giving me the mental respite from my, then rather harrowing, personal circumstances I had hoped it would, so I persevered. Another problem, I had no formal training as an academic historian and had to learn to research my subjects as I went along, which I soon found was positively advantageous since I was able to look at events from an entirely new angle and often found that my own reading of the behaviour of our remote ancestors was at variance with the traditionalist view. I pressed on regardless.

As the end of 1995 approached I was fast "running down" to Bosworth. En route, I had devised a new way of illustrating the course of a battle, which I felt made events much clearer than any established method I had seen, decided on a title: "The Hollow Crowns" [who needs another book called "The Wars of the Roses"?] which gave me the idea for the cover design and was feeling rather more like I imagined a successful author should. And then I hit a snag.

I had never been able to work out, to my own satisfaction, two events in the story of Richard III's brief reign. On the murder of the Princes in the Tower, having read Josephine Tey in my youth, I felt there was an equal chance that this murky deed was inspired by Henry VII as by Richard, so no particular problem there. On the other hand, I could not understand why he should have butchered – there is no other word for it – Lord William Hastings as he did, nor could I ever rationalise Buckingham deserting a king he had helped to his throne only three months previously and rising in rebellion against him.

I ploughed through ancient notes and photocopied pages yet again in search of the enlightenment I wanted to convey through my final inter-chapter and was suddenly struck by a phrase, three words long, in a passage copied from More's Historie, relating to the aftermath of the Strawberries Meeting in the White Tower. It told how – apart from Hastings – the participants had been dealt with, and there I saw that John Morton, Bishop of Ely, inventor of Morton's Fork and right-hand of Henry VII had been sent to confinement in Brecknock Castle, Buckingham's favourite seat, "at Buckingham's request". Three words I had read many times and never really understood. And, for the first time, I asked myself: "Why? " And light began to dawn until, two days later, I had all the answers, including who had really been responsible for the murder of the Princes and when and why.

Now what do I do? I had a completely new, totally logical solution, to what Paul Kendall refers to as "The most celebrated mystery in the annals of England" and nowhere to put it. It did not fit into the history I had set out to produce and I couldn't bring myself to "chuck it away" – my initial reaction. In the end, I wrote it as an appendix, called it "Who Killed the King? " and went contentedly on to "do" Bosworth and the end of "The Hollow Crowns".

I then – as I had always intended to do – designed and published the book myself and, after a deal of hard work, found it sold quite successfully. The only problem was that the appendix seemed to arouse as much interest as the main body of the book and, cut to the chase, I ended up writing and publishing another volume. The second opus considerably expanded on the account of the Princes' murder and included new discoveries on the schemes of three people, which had changed the course of English history, people I called "The Deceivers".

Having finished my second [unplanned] work, I looked forward to a more restful retirement than I had known to then. Unhappily – or perhaps, not so – the ladies at Middleham Castle had different ideas and, in short order, I found myself writing, at their request, the "first ever history" of the Middleham Nevilles, which came out in the summer of 1998 as "The Lordly Ones". And thence, it was but a short step to another "first ever": the history of the Woodville family, which became "The Popinjays", and was the first medieval history to be published in England during the year 2000.

Finally, [I think] I wrote this history, after being reminded that I had always wanted to write the first-ever book on the Beauforts. There was a residual suggestion as well: that I might then combine all five books in some way into the definitive history of the Wars of the Roses. In fact, I believe this may have happened "accidentally", since, as I have gone deeper into their story, I have come to realise that the history of the Beauforts is the whole history of the conflict between York and Lancaster. Without them and their pride of blood, England might well have been a greener and pleasanter land and, as they say, the whole history of the World would have been different.

Arms of the Beauforts,
the 'Bordure' indicates the family's legitimation.

Prologue

"Genesis"

Richard II

(Detail from the w.w.w.)

"GENESIS"

"Begin at the beginning, the King said...
go on till you come to the end: then stop."
[Alice in Wonderland]

On a day in March in the year of our Lord 1340, in the Flanders' town of Ghent, Philippa of Hainault, Queen to Edward III – King of England, Lord of Ireland, and claimant to the throne of France – gave birth to her fourth male child. The new Prince was christened John and, in accordance with the custom, was further distinguished, in common parlance, by having the name of his birthplace added to his given name. English tongues did not happily wrap themselves around the word Ghent, but easily adapted the sound into their own vernacular. Thus it would be that, as John of Gaunt, the new arrival would eventually carve a turbulent path through the history of England, France, and Spain during his near-sixty years of life.

At the age of nineteen, in May 1359, John married Blanche of Lancaster, Countess in her own right of Derby and, with her elder sister, the wealthiest heiress in England. Their first child, Philippa, who was born on the last day of March in the year following, would become Queen of Portugal through her marriage with King John, and a second daughter, Elizabeth, followed some four years later and in due time married John Holland and became Duchess of Exeter.

In the intervening period between the two births, Gaunt and his older brother Lionel of Antwerp were created Dukes of Lancaster and Clarence respectively, benefiting from the prosperity of England, which stemmed equally from French booty, the increasingly rich trade in English wool, and the desire of their father, King Edward, to maintain and increase the prestige of his family. Subsequently, Blanche's union with John of Gaunt produced five more children of which four were boys, but the only male child to survive infancy, born on the 30th of May, 1366, was Henry, later known as Henry Bolingbroke, Earl of Derby, who would become Henry IV of England after usurping his cousin Richard's throne and murdering him in the last year of the fourteenth century.

Initially, however, it is the daughters born to Gaunt and Blanche of Lancaster with whom we must concern ourselves. Unlike their brothers, the two girls seem to have been very healthy, Philippa living to 55 years of age, and Elizabeth to 61. They both married well and fruitfully, Philippa producing 11 children including a King of Portugal and the famous explorer, Prince Henry the Navigator, while Elizabeth married three times in all, first to John Hastings, Earl of Pembroke when she was 16, annulled three years later, then to the Duke of Exeter by whom she bore five children and finally – when nearing 40 – to the original "boy next door", a John Cornwall of Burford, first Baron Fanhope, by whom she had a further son and daughter.

Blanche was less fortunate than her girls. Repeated attempts to provide the son and heir Gaunt needed to found his own particular part of the royal dynasty proved abortive and weakening and, in any event, it was customary to appoint a governess to carry some of the burden of basic education of the daughters of princes. By 1366, a suitable candidate had been found in the shape of Katherine, the 16 year old younger daughter of Sir Payne Roelt, a knight of Hainault who had come to England in the train of Queen Philippa and who held the office of Guyenne, King of arms.

Within a year of her appointment, Katherine was married to Sir Hugh Swynford, a Lincolnshire knight, who held his lands at Coleby from the Duke of Lancaster and who served John of Gaunt in military matters. Shortly after the marriage, in the year 1366, Hugh Swynford received letters of protection, as being in the retinue of John of Gaunt in Gascony and there, beyond seas, he died "on the Thursday after St Martin", November 13th, 1371. There is no record of him having returned to England during his service in France, which may be accounted strange, since Katherine Swynford bore a son, Thomas, in 1368 and a daughter, Dorothy, had also appeared by 1370. John of Gaunt stood as godfather to the girl at her christening – a signal mark of honour which would cost him dear in the matter of a Papal dispensation in years to come.

Blanche of Lancaster died, a victim of the Black Death, on September 12th 1368 and, within three years, John of Gaunt had achieved a life-long ambition and acquired the title of King, through his marriage to Constance, Queen of Castile, daughter of Pedro the Cruel. This second marriage lasted 23 years, until Constance's death in Leicester Castle, but produced only two children: Katherine of Lancaster, later Queen of Castile through her marriage to King Henry and a boy, John, born like his father in Ghent, but who did not survive infancy.

Meantime, following the death of Hugh Swynford, his widow Katherine obtained a grant of two thirds of the land her husband had held at Coleby by payment of a fee of £20 to the King. Richard II had also assumed responsibility for the marriage arrangements of Thomas Swynford, who would remain a royal ward until he came of age. Signal honours again for the son of an undistinguished knight who had died in the service of his Liege-lord in a land "beyond seas". During the same period, Katherine also came into possession of the Manor of Kettlethorpe, apparently for her own lifetime, since she was generally known locally henceforth as the Lady of Kettlethorpe.

Again, it was about this time, according to common report, that the Lady Katherine became the mistress of John of Gaunt and by her he had a further four children, three boys and a girl. The four took the name of Beaufort from the castle in Anjou, which formed part of their father's vast estates. They also inherited his undying hunger for power and wealth, which dominated Gaunt's entire life and which his bastard brood duly passed on to their own issue, genetically and by example. This would have dire effects on the history of the "scept'red isle" which the Duke of Lancaster, according to the Bard, discussed with his brother, the Duke of York, at Ely House in London, during his final illness.

The four first-born Beauforts arrived at two-yearly intervals from 1373 to 1379 and, two years after the death of Constance, Gaunt felt able, in 1396, to make legal his long-term association with Katherine. The eldest son, John Beaufort, was created first Earl of Somerset in the following year, in which, he and his siblings, at Gaunt's urgent request and following Papal dispensation of the "marital" link through Gaunt's godfatherhood of the Swynford daughter, were legitimated by Richard II. Henry IV subsequently confirmed the legitimation early in his reign, with a hand-written qualification indicating that no right to succeed to the crown was to be conveyed thereby.

The second Beaufort son, Henry, was destined for the church and became wealthy, first as a Bishop and then Cardinal, playing a dominant role in the ruling of England as Chancellor in 1403-05 and again in 1413-17 and 1424-26. A third son, Thomas, was created Duke of Exeter and also rose to high office, Admiral, Chancellor of England, Ambassador to France, but he married unexceptionally and had only one son who died young. He died himself short of his fiftieth year, and his life, so full of early promise, ultimately left few footprints in the sands of time. Would that his siblings had done likewise.

The youngest of the family – and the only girl – was Joan who, after a brief first marriage to Robert, Lord Ferrers, became the second wife of that most uxorious of Earls, Ralph Neville of Westmorland, by whom she had fourteen children, including Richard Neville, Earl of Salisbury and father to the Kingmaker, and Cecily Neville, the Rose of Raby, mother of Edward IV and Richard III. And, while Joan seems to have been a loving daughter to Katherine and a loyal, supportive and exceedingly fruitful wife to Earl Ralph, she was also acquisitive and strong-willed, and conveyed in full measure to her children and grandchildren the blood-royal and the driving ambition she had inherited from her own father.

During her twenty-five years as Gaunt's mistress, Katherine showed herself, not unnaturally, as having her own share of acquisitive traits of character. She received regular gifts of property and land from the Duke and seems to have had the run of Gaunt's house in Lincoln High Street. She regularly extended her properties at Coleby and Kettlethorpe through the purchase of small parcels of land and property in and adjacent to them at Laughterton and Fenton. She also looked to the wool trade for improvements in her income and, in 1383 for example, had license from the King to enclose and make a park in 300 acres of land and woods within her Manor of Kettlethorpe. Enclosures always resulted in the expulsion of small farmers previously renting the land and often caused rioting and vandalism on the part of the dispossessed.

So it was in Katherine's case, where a commission of oyer and terminer was issued on the 17th of August 1384 and again on the 20th of September of that year, against sundry men of Lincoln, including John Saltby, the Mayor of the town, for breaking the Lady of Kettlethorpe's close, taking her goods and assaulting her servants. Such assaults no doubt ceased when, following the death of his second wife, John of Gaunt married Katherine in Lincoln Cathedral on January 13th 1396, for the new Duchess of Lancaster would not be considered a suitable target for retributory raids, however well-deserved these might be.

The marriage was not to last long, "time-honoured Lancaster" was already in his mid fifties when he took his vows for the third time and concern at the exile shortly afterwards of his only legitimately-born son, Henry Bolingbroke, did much to impair Gaunt's increasingly frail constitution. He died on February 3rd, 1399 and his final legacy to his country – "...this other Eden, demi-Paradise...", to the English people "...this happy breed of men..." and to his own House, the Plantagenets, "...royal kings, fear'd by their breed, and famous by their birth..." was the seeds of thirty years of warfare, which would utterly destroy the last, and lengthily and seriously harm the first two. Those seeds would germinate and blossom in the second generation of Beauforts, the Royal Bastards, who could never – would never – forget that they were born of Kings.

Katherine Swynford outlived the Duke of Lancaster by little more than four years and was buried during the month of May 1403 in Lincoln Cathedral, with her second son, Henry Beaufort, who was then Bishop, reading the offices.

Katherine Swynford

(Drawing from an 18th century treatise)

**Effigy of John Beaufort, 1st Earl of Somerset,
Canterbury Cathedral**
(G. Wheeler)

Part One

The
Harbingers

CHAPTER ONE

The King's Man

John Beaufort was created first Earl of Somerset in February 1397, when he was 23 years old and later in the same year, further advantage followed through his marriage to the wealthy heiress, and cousin to the King himself, Margaret Holland. Somerset then demonstrated his attachment to Richard's party when joining with seven other Lords Appellant in laying a Bill before Parliament by which Thomas of Woodstock, Duke of Gloucester and the King's uncle, with Richard Fitzalan, the very wealthy Earl of Arundel, whom King Richard regarded as his most deadly enemy and had struck in the face when Fitzalan arrived late for the Queen's funeral, and Thomas Beauchamp, Earl of Warwick, were condemned of treason. Arundel was executed and Warwick sent into exile, as was Arundel's brother, Thomas, Archbishop of Canterbury. Thomas of Woodstock was already dead, murdered by Richard's order in Calais Castle.

Following Richard's triumph over those he saw as his main enemies, it was time to reward the Lords who had stood his friends and supporters and five dukedoms were created, including that of Hereford for Henry Bolingbroke, Norfolk for Thomas Mowbray, and Exeter for the King's half-brother, John Holland, while on John Beaufort, already Earl of Somerset, Gaunt's oldest child by Katherine Swynford, was bestowed the Marquessate of Dorset. Four new Earldoms also appeared including that of Westmorland for Ralph Neville, Lord of Middleham and Raby, and Thomas Percy, brother to Henry, Earl of Northumberland, became Earl of Worcester.

The hoped-for assurance of loyalty from some of the country's most powerful magnates, now further aggrandised, was short-lived. In January 1398, Henry Bolingbroke, new-made Duke of Hereford, appeared in the Parliament, and accused Mowbray, new Duke of Norfolk, of treasonous utterances suggesting that the King planned to deal with the two of them as he had already with Arundel and Thomas of Woodstock. These accusations, denied by Norfolk, were sent for investigation by two select committees, which, after lengthy consideration, were unable to decide where the truth lay between the two Dukes. Therefore, in accordance with ancient custom, they were commanded to settle the dispute by personal combat, which was set to take place at Coventry on September 16th.

In the event, as soon as Norfolk and Hereford appeared in the lists, the King ordered them to desist and condemned them to exile, Mowbray for life and his cousin for ten years. Clearly, Richard was unable to risk the outcome of the duel – if Norfolk triumphed it would appear that his accusations against Richard had been true and, were Bolingbroke to win, it would add further laurels to the reputation of one sufficiently close to the throne to make him a credible successor in the event of his outliving Richard.

Just over four months later, on February 3rd 1399, John of Gaunt, Duke of Lancaster, one-time King of Castile and Leon, and, after the King his nephew, the greatest man in England, died in Leicester Castle. Some said he died of a broken heart following the exile of his son and heir, but he had reached a ripe old age at the end of a very active life and, with no more worlds to try to conquer, he had little purpose in extending his days any further. Whatever the reason, Lancaster was dead and the strongest, most-enduring pillar of Richard's reign was removed.

The King moved quickly to counter the threat he perceived must now come from the new head of the House of Lancaster, Henry Bolingbroke. A meeting of his inner cabinet on March 18th agreed to extend Hereford's sentence of banishment from ten years to life and, although Gaunt's bequests to his Duchess, Katherine, were honoured, the bulk of Gaunt's estates was parcelled out amongst Richard's strongest supporters, in particular, his half-brothers, the Dukes of Exeter and Surrey, and his cousin, Edward, Duke of Aumale. Thus, at a stroke, King Richard ensured that his cousin, Bolingbroke, must spend the rest of his life in exiled penury, if he could not recover his titles, lands and wealth by force of arms. He should have had few illusions as to which course the turbulent Duke of Hereford would take.

Unhappily for him, Richard II, throughout his reign, had become progressively ever more assured of his absolute right to rule as he pleased in his own lands. Capricious, with the Plantagenet temper in full measure and continually surrounded by fawning favourites and protected by the strong arms of his bodyguard of Cheshire archers, the King seemed uncaring, unaware even, of the dangers implicit in the course he had chosen. In May came news of a new revolt by Art McMurrough, most intransigent of the Irish chieftains, which King Richard decided he would put down himself and early in June he sailed for Ireland. The King left his surviving uncle, the ancient and ineffective Duke of York, as Protector of the realm, and took the additional precaution of transporting much of the royal treasure with him as well as the sons of Hereford and Thomas of Woodstock, who would make useful hostages should such occasion arise.

In the latter move, he showed some forethought at least, since early in July, Henry Bolingbroke landed at the fishing port of Ravenspur at Humbermouth with a small force of English troops and moved quickly on to Pontefract Castle. Here, by pre-arrangement, he was joined by Henry Percy, Earl of Northumberland, with his son, the famed soldier, Harry Hotspur, and by the tall, limping figure of Ralph Neville, Earl of Westmorland by the grace of King Richard but, by his second marriage to Joan Beaufort, half brother-in-law to Bolingbroke as well. Both Earls brought strong forces with them and, as Bolingbroke moved quickly southwards, men flocked to join his standard. The seeds of hatred that the only son of the Black Prince had sewed through much of the previous 22 years were ripening rapidly and yielding a brimming crop of vengeance.

With no firm central authority to lead and inspire those forces loyal to the King, the rebel army met little resistance. Protector York had taken refuge from the coming onslaught in Berkeley Castle in Gloucestershire and meekly surrendered it to Bolingbroke when summoned. Taking York with them, the rebels swept on to Bristol where the main leaders of the royal inner cabinet had taken refuge while awaiting their King's return from Ireland. York was obliged to summon the garrison to capitulate and this they did, surrendering Richard's chief lieutenants, Sir John Bussy and Sir Henry Green to Bolingbroke. Both were summarily executed at Bristol on July 29th.

Two days prior to the death of his strongest adherents, Richard II had sailed from Ireland with a strong force of men. Unhappily for him, he was badly advised by his cousin Aumale and the newly installed Earl of Worcester, Thomas Percy, and decided to split his army. Montagu, Earl of Salisbury was sent with a strong force to north Wales to raise further support there, meantime Richard himself landed in the south of the Principality, basing his army at Haverfordwest, from where heralds were sent through Glamorgan and the surrounding counties to raise support. When no reinforcement arrived, the

King's army started to dwindle and he was persuaded by Aumale and Worcester to abandon the south and concentrate all his efforts with Salisbury's northern force.

By this time, Bolingbroke was being kept well-informed of Richard's plans by Aumale and Thomas Percy and pre-empted the King's move towards the loyal estates in Cheshire, entering Chester on August 9th. Richard reached Conway two days later where he found Salisbury holding the castle with barely a hundred men left of his original force. There was no option for the King but to treat and Richard duly gave audience to Northumberland and Archbishop Arundel when they appeared and agreed terms. Bolingbroke would have his rights to the Lancaster inheritance fully restored and Northumberland swore on the Host that Richard should retain his crown.

Richard, with his small, surviving retinue left Conway for London and was captured in an ambuscade and taken before Bolingbroke in Chester. From here writs were sent out under Richard's seal for a Parliament on August 19th at Westminster and the cousins set out together for London, where Richard was placed in the Tower. A deputation of the City Fathers meantime attended on Bolingbroke, advising him that they had withdrawn their fealty to Richard and commending London to the care of the Duke of Lancaster.

Knowing Richard's inclination to deceit and his deep-seated vengeful qualities, Bolingbroke realised there was no turning back – if he had ever believed that an accommodation with his royal cousin would be possible – and after some weeks of tortuous negotiations with and through Parliament, Richard "resigned" his crown. In evidence of this, Bollingbroke displayed the King's signet "which had been given to him" and the Duke of Lancaster went on to claim the throne on grounds of his descent from Edmund Crouchback, son of Henry III, "and through the right that God of His grace hath sent me, with the help of my kin and my friends to recover it". The reign of Henry IV of England was held to have commenced on September 30th 1399.

In view of the method by which his crown had been acquired, Henry's coronation was held early in his reign, on October 13th, St Edward's Day. The first Parliament of his regime began business proper the day after the crowning of the new King and concentrated much of its early days in repealing legislation passed in the last three years of Richard's rule. Thus Arundel was restored to his Archbishopric of Canterbury, Thomas Fitzalan to his dead father's dignity and estate of Arundel and Thomas Beauchamp, Earl

Henry IV

(Detail from the w.w.w.)

of Warwick, was called home from exile.

A form of trial of the previous King's closest advisers and supporters was undertaken, the main hearings being held in secret, and the outcome was lenient in the extreme. Richard's half-brothers, John and Thomas Holland were deprived of their ducal titles and reverted to their Earldoms. The same treatment was applied to Aumale since, although he admitted primary responsibility for the murder of Thomas of Woodstock in Calais, he escaped the customary punishment by the novel, possibly unique, plea in such cases of "force majeure"- the King had ordered him to do it. In the same way, John Beaufort lost his title of Marquess of Dorset, reverting to the less-distinguished rank of Earl of Somerset, to which, on November 9th, his new King and half-brother added the title of Chamberlain of England.

With the establishment of his dynasty through the investiture of his eldest son, Henry, as Prince of Wales, Duke of Cornwall and Earl of Chester, the last link in Lancaster's chain around the monarchy was the disposal of the former ruler. On October 21st the Commons petitioned that Richard should be called to answer for the misdeeds alleged against him and two days later, 58 Lords Temporal and Spiritual, including John Beaufort, and sitting in secret session, advised that the former King should be condemned to perpetual imprisonment in a secret place. On October 28th, he was moved, heavily disguised, from the Tower via Leeds Castle in Kent, to Pontefract, where his immediate custodians were Robert Waterton and Sir Thomas Swynford, who would later become Captain of Calais and was said by some to be an unacknowledged offspring of John of Gaunt and, thereby, half-brother to Henry IV.

Richard's fate was finally sealed by a rebellion of his former supporters led by his half-brothers, the plans for which were betrayed by the former Duke of Aumale, now Earl of Rutland again, through his father, the Duke of York. Henry, with his sons, and the help of the people of London, swiftly raised an army of 20,000, scattered the rebels and caught their leaders at Cirencester. Initially promised their lives pending interviews with the King, Thomas Holland, Earl of Kent and half-brother to Richard, and John Montagu, Earl of Salisbury, unwittingly providing a precursor to the fate of another Salisbury 60 years later, were both seized by "an angry mob" and beheaded in the streets of Cirencester. Lord Despenser, deprived of his former honour as Earl of Gloucester, met a similar fate in Bristol days later. John

Holland, Earl of Huntingdon, was even more unfortunate than his brother, being captured by men of the Countess of Hereford, sister to the late Earl of Arundel and mother-in-law to the equally late Duke of Gloucester. Holland was handed over to the vengeful men of Essex and his end was hard indeed.

With the failure of the rebellion, Richard's own fate was sealed and he was killed in Pontefract Castle during the last two weeks of January 1400. To prevent circulation of rumours of his survival, his body was carried to London and exposed at various places en route to St Paul's, where the new King attended the funeral mass, acting as a pall-bearer. The corpse was transferred to King's Langley in Hertfordshire, where it was buried in the presence of the Bishop of Lichfield and the Abbots of St Albans and Waltham.

Henry Bolingbroke would rule England for thirteen years after Richard's death and his three half-brothers all achieved high office during his reign. John Beaufort had the offer from Parliament of reinstatement in his former dignity of Marquess of Dorset, but he declined and so it was that, as Earl of Somerset, he became Chamberlain of England and Captain of Calais. The high Offices held by the three brothers brought them into regular and close contact with their nephew, Prince Hal, the future Henry V. A particular example was the appointment of the Prince of Wales as Constable of Dover and Warden of the Cinque Ports at the end of February 1409, necessitating regular liaison between Henry and John Beaufort who commanded for England on the other side of the Channel crossing.

The closeness of the Beauforts' relationship with the Prince, and with their half-brother, King Henry, had been further evidenced earlier, on February 10th 1407, when the legitimation of all the progeny of John of Gaunt's long-lasting relationship with Katherine Swynford was confirmed by Henry IV, who, however, personally inserted a clause into the Parliamentary Act excluding the possibility of the Beaufort line ever succeeding to the crown. They would walk with kings, do battle for and with kings, live with and like kings, but they might not become kings – royal unquestionably, regal never.

The matter of royal succession denied did not trouble John Beaufort, first Earl of Somerset, for any great length of time, since he died, still short of his fortieth year, on March 14th, 1410. He left behind a young family of three boys and two girls from his fruitful marriage to Margaret Holland, daughter of the Earl of Kent, two of whom would convey the blood royal to a third generation, whose involvement in England's history would have dire results for a century. On these grounds, it may be accounted fortunate that there was no continuing of the Beaufort line through his two brothers. However, this was more than compensated by the abundantly productive family-branch stemming from the Earl's only sister, Joan, whose marriage to Ralph Neville, the prolific Earl of Westmorland, would produce more major-part players for the impending drama, than all the others put together.

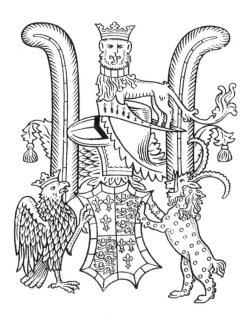

Coat of Arms of John Beaufort, Duke of Somerset

(G. Wheeler)

CHAPTER TWO

A Man of Much Promise

John Beaufort's youngest brother, Thomas, was four years his junior, born in 1377 and, like his siblings, spent his early formative years at the castle of Beaufort near Angers. He was nineteen when his parents married and in the following year was ennobled as Earl of Dorset. Following the usurpation of the throne by his half-brother, Henry Bolingbroke, Thomas became a close friend of the young Prince Hal and rode with him in his successful campaigns against the Welsh.

He supported Prince Henry through his political friction with the Prince's younger brother, Thomas of Clarence and his ally, Thomas Fitzalan, Archbishop of Canterbury and Chancellor of England, and Thomas Beaufort was named Chancellor in January 1410, following Fitzalan's forced resignation a month earlier. This gave Thomas a seat in the new inner Council on which his brilliant brother, Henry, now Bishop of Winchester also took a place. Thus the family fortunes continued to rise ever higher despite the death two months later of John, Earl of Somerset.

The political dominance of Prince Hal and the Beauforts was maintained for two years, but then was sharply reversed due to a combination of factors. The root cause was the virtual civil war in France, where Burgundy and Armagnac struggled to dominate a weak King, and this combined with the failing health of Henry IV, culminating in an ill-timed suggestion from Henry Beaufort that the King should relinquish the throne in favour of his eldest son. For much of 1411, a major expedition had been planned to protect England's possessions in Gascony and around Calais from French depredations, and to recover lost territory in Aquitaine, and Henry IV had intended to lead the undertaking. However, when the force was ready to set sail at the end of September, it was clear the King was not fit to command it in what could well be an arduous campaign and Beaufort, ever the political opportunist, proposed the change to a younger, fitter leader.

Unfortunately for him, and for the Prince of Wales' fortunes as well, the King, while undoubtedly sick unto death, was a long way still from the final portal and made his displeasure – and his continuing power – immediately clear. A Parliament was called for November at which the Prince and his main supporters were thanked for their services in the King's Council and replaced by royal nominees. Among the losers was Thomas Beaufort who on December 19th was required to return the Chancellor's seal to his immediate predecessor, Archbishop Arundel.

In the summer of the following year, after extended – and separate – negotiations with the Dukes of Burgundy and Armagnac, a strong English force commanded by the King's second son, Thomas of Clarence, and including a contingent of 240 men-at-arms and 700 archers led by Thomas Beaufort, embarked for France. On landing, they found that their expected support from Armagnac had evaporated, following a grand reconciliation between the competing French nobles and that they would have to fight their corner unaided. However, they were a strong force and advanced through Anjou towards Blois, whence they moved on towards Orleans. The French Dukes were, by now, keen to buy off the invaders and since their offers were generous and the campaigning season was coming to an end, Clarence accepted the indemnity of gold and jewels he was offered and passed on into Gascony intending to overwinter at Bordeaux and renew his campaign in the following spring.

This he did but as he commenced his advance against French forces commanded by Armagnac, news arrived of the death of his father on March 20th 1413 and Clarence retired again on Bordeaux and sailed immediately for England.

Harry of Monmouth was crowned Henry V, King of England, in Westminster Abbey on April 9th 1413. He was 25 years old and had spent half his life in camp and field serving his King and his country. He had learned the arts of war from lengthy campaigns against Owen Glendower, the last great general of the Welsh, and from fighting with, and against, Harry Percy, known better as "Hotspur", the fiercest and most experienced English commander of his time. Denied leadership of the most recent English expedition to France, the new King was eager to take an army across the Channel to reclaim his rights and lands there, but first he would try diplomacy.

He sent requests of the King of France, in proper form, for formal redress of England's wrongs and waited several months on the French reply. When this came in the June of 1414, it was delivered through an embassy led by the Archbishop of Bourges, who indicated that King Charles was quite amenable to making minor concessions within the Duchy of Guienne. But, when Henry raised the question of restoration of the Duchies of Normandy and Guienne, and the Counties of Anjou and Poitou, Maine, Touraine and Ponthieu, which, he said, were his by right of his claim to the crown of France, the Archbishop made him a very plain reply. He said, "Sire, the King of France our Sovereign Lord is the true King of France, nor have you any right to these things you claim, nor to the Kingdom of England [which] belongs to the true heirs of King Richard, nor can our Sovereign Lord safely treat [further] with you."

Henry was, at once, angered and astonished by this reply, which effectively brought negotiations to an end. He gave the ambassadors safe conduct for the return voyage to their homeland, where, he said, they might look for him to follow closely on their heels. Before leaving, some of the French party sought news from sympathetic sources close to the English throne and learned that a secret treaty of alliance had been concluded with Burgundy on May 23rd which would be implemented on Henry's landing in France to reclaim his crown.

When the Archbishop and his party had left, King Henry immediately set preparations on foot for a full-scale invasion of France. For months England buzzed in anticipation of the coming venture until on March 22nd 1415, Henry issued a formal proclamation by which all soldiers owing the King service, by reason of fiefs or wages, were to rendezvous in London. This was followed a month later by a great War-council at which Henry appointed his brother, John, Duke of Bedford, as Regent in England during the royal absence.

With preparations virtually completed, the grand expedition was nearly rendered leaderless before it commenced through a conspiracy led by Richard, Earl of Cambridge, close kin to the Yorkist heir to the throne, aided and abetted by Lord Scrope, Treasurer of England and Sir Thomas Gray a knight from the north country. Bribed with French gold, these three had pledged to assassinate the King with a view to the Yorkists seizing the throne thereafter, but their plot was discovered and they paid the price of their treachery at the beginning of August 1415. On Sunday, August 11th Henry gave the signal and a fleet of 1,500 vessels began to move out past Spithead and down the Channel towards France. The ships carried, in addition to supplies of every kind and ancillary personnel from surgeons to minstrels and fiddlers, 65 gunners, 2,000 men-at-arms and 8,000 archers.

Heading the fleet was the King's uncle and appointed-admiral, Thomas Beaufort, Earl of Dorset, who proudly led this great armada past the Isle of Wight and down-channel, heading south for the French coast. At his masthead, Dorset carried two lanterns as guiding beacons for the ships to follow. The great adventure had begun.

The army enjoyed a smooth crossing and came to anchor in the mouth of the Seine during the late afternoon of August 14th, three miles from their first objective, the port of Harfleur, "the key to France". Disembarkation commenced on the morning following, under the supervision of Thomas Beaufort and three days later the troops and all their impedimenta lay in a great camp on a hill to the northwest of Harfleur. Henry decided the port was too strong to take by storm and, instead, concentrated on surrounding the town and wearing the defence down by using his miners and artillery. By September 19th, the garrison had reached the end of their resources under regular assaults by the English force and agreed to surrender after three more days if the Dauphin's army did not relieve them. And so it was that, on September 22nd 1415, the Lord de Gaucourt, commander of the town of Harfleur, surrendered to Henry V his first conquest in France. He, and his captains with the town's civic dignitaries, 76 men in all, appeared before their new master with rope halters around their necks, as their predecessors, the Burghers of Calais, had done some 70 years earlier when they surrendered to Edward III.

Having established his new base, Henry called a council of war to decide his next move. Three courses were open to him. He could continue to advance on Paris, though the campaigning season was now much further advanced than he had counted on; he could over-winter in Harfleur and strengthen his hold on the town by adding neighbouring territory to the "Pale", or he could make a Grande Chevauchée as his great-uncle, the Black

Prince, had done years before, and march his army through the lands usurped by the King of France back to Calais and thence to England.

Although the force available to him had been reduced from its original size by casualties and – mainly – by dysentery, there was never much doubt as to which course he would take and, on October 8th, the army of Henry V marched out of Harfleur towards Arques, 6,000 men on the first stage of their route to Calais and, though they could not know it, at the beginning of their road into the pages of military Legend. He left behind a strong garrison of 1,200 archers and 900 men-at arms to hold Harfleur under the reliable command of his uncle, Thomas Beaufort.

Garter Stall Plate of Thomas Beaufort,
Duke of Exeter.

(G. Wheeler)

CHAPTER THREE

"Tell your master that Englishmen do not surrender!"

T he Earl of Dorset, denied the honour of participating in England's most stunning victory in France, occupied himself and his garrison usefully while his King was winning timeless glory at Agincourt, by repairing the defences of the town, recruiting English artisans and merchants to settle in this "new Calais" and raiding the surrounding countryside regularly to ensure food and fodder supplies. One of his leading commanders of these raiding parties was a John Fastolf, who thereby learned much of the trade-skills he was to apply so signally in later campaigns.

In the January of 1416, the original garrison was relieved and the occupying force enlarged to a total of 2,500 men, more than half of which were archers. Dorset accompanied the returning troops to England to enjoy a few weeks rest and settle his own affairs and by the beginning of March was back again in command of Harfleur. On the 9th of that month, he led a force of 1,000 men-at-arms and archers, all mounted, on a three-day raid northeast towards Picardy. They gathered supplies and booty on their way to the town of Cany, some miles south of St Valery, looted and burned it and turned southwest again for Harfleur.

They had travelled only three miles when they passed through a village called Ouainville and were spotted by French scouts who alerted their main force to the approach of the English. Five miles further along their road home, and nearing the village of Valmont, Dorset's men were badly surprised to find their way blocked by around 4,000 French cavalry led by the newly-made Constable of France, Bernard of Armagnac. Dorset, realising an attack was imminent, followed standard English tactics in such circumstances by dismounting his entire force, and sending horses and baggage wagons to the rear. He then arrayed his force in a single line stretched as far as it would go to secure reliable cover for his flanks.

The stretching process, however, made the English line very thin in parts and repeated French cavalry charges ultimately broke through at several

Henry V

(Detail from the w.w.w.)

points. This should have spelled the end of English resistance with their attackers wheeling right and left behind the line and finishing off any remaining opposition. The French, however, continued to charge straight forward, making for the unguarded baggage wagons bulging with the loot from Dorset's raid, which they proceeded to pillage after cutting down the unarmed grooms and boy attendants, as their countrymen had done barely six months earlier at Agincourt.

Dorset took full advantage of this unexpected breathing space by leading his dismounted troops into a large garden which he had used initially to protect his flank and there forming square behind the hedges and ditches which surrounded the cultivated area. The Comte d' Armagnac, having recalled his men to their duty, examined the new English position carefully and the more he saw of it the less he liked it. He therefore sent emissaries to try to persuade the English to surrender and, while Dorset – having been wounded himself during the fight and with 150 casualties already – was not averse to calling a truce and returning to Harfleur empty-handed, Armagnac required the surrender of the entire English force. This Dorset dismissed, in terms strangely similar to those supposedly used centuries later by remnants of Napoleon's last Armée at Waterloo, ordering the heralds to "Tell your master that Englishmen do not surrender!"

Armagnac decided to sleep on it and with the bulk of his force withdrew into Valmont for food and rest. Thomas Beaufort, noting the lack of sentries in his immediate vicinity, commenced a silent withdrawal and made a night-march to Fécamp, seven miles to the west, then turning south for another seven miles to a wood at Les Loges, where he decided to rest his weary men since dawn was now breaking. Armagnac realised his mistake when he advanced on the garden position and immediately sent strong troops of horsemen west and south seeking for his vanished opponents. In this they were unsuccessful and as darkness fell, Dorset continued to lead his men south towards the sea coast with the intention of taking them back into Harfleur along the beach and into the Seine estuary, marching alongside the water all the way, to guard his right flank.

It seemed that the ploy was working and the English were virtually within sight of Harfleur, at the foot of the cliffs of St Andress, when they were seen from a hill above the track by a large force of enemy cavalry. The French leaped from their horses and charged down the precipitous slope on foot; they would kill the English raiders, or drive them drowning into the river mouth. But the English footmen had had enough of being driven and killed. They had a short space in which to form a rough line and this they did; the French arrived piecemeal and winded by their race down the crag to where the English waited with their axes and long knives. The triumphing French were cut down in detail and the victors stripped their corpses and threw the remains into the Seine.

All was not yet done, for, as the victorious English formed up to continue their march into Harfleur, the main French body of cavalry, led by Bernard of Armagnac, appeared on the heights above the track leading directly to the safe haven they had sought for so many weary miles. Salvation it seemed was to be denied at the very last moment of their arduous adventure. However, once more: enough was enough. Invigorated by their recent victory, Dorset's footmen were to perform even greater prodigies of valour in seizing their axes, knives and spears and charging up the steep face of the hill into the astonished French. Armagnac and his men waited for no more – they broke and fled for Rouen as fast as their horses' legs could carry them.

Unhappily for them, their road led past Harfleur where the garrison had been alerted by the sounds of battle and had arrayed themselves accordingly. As the fleeing French passed the town, they were met by a furious sortie in which the garrison killed many and took still more prisoner. The English triumph of Valmont/Harfleur was complete; it was not as great as Agincourt, nor as far-reaching in its political effects, but, as an exhibition of dogged courage reversing a potentially catastrophic defeat to snatch a near-impossible victory, it has few, if any, equals in the annals of warfare.

Thomas Beaufort had been sorely wounded during the fighting but continued in his command of the Harfleur garrison. His exploits against Armagnac had made clear to the French leadership the significance of English occupation of the port and, in addition to a renewed siege from the landward side, they hired a number of great, fighting carracks from the Genoese and from Navarre and blockaded the outlet to the Seine. Harfleur was completely cut off from its supply base and the garrison of the town soon began to suffer the usual effects: hunger, disease and consequent drop in morale. Beaufort wrote to the King in London, where he was discussing a possible peace initiative with the German Emperor, Sigismund, setting out his dire need for supplies of all sorts, especially horses and guns.

An initial convoy failed to get through the French blockade and, with the arrival of further pleas for support from Dorset, Henry realised a major effort must be made if Harfleur was to remain in English hands. As quickly as possible, a great fleet of close on 100 ships was assembled which Henry was unable to command himself being still deeply involved in negotiations with the Emperor. He therefore ordered his second brother, John of Bedford, to lead the fleet to the relief of Harfleur and early in the morning of August 14th, with a fair wind for France, the armada set sail from its rendezvous anchorage off Beachy Head.

The fleet made a swift crossing and in the evening of the same day came to anchor in the mouth of the Seine. Bedford sent rowing boats into the river during the night to reconnoitre the enemy fleet's dispositions and the scouts found their adversaries anchored together in the centre of the estuary, roughly midway between Harfleur and Honfleur. The morning breeze came from the northwest and, discarding any thoughts of skilled manoeuvring for which there was little scope in the waters of the estuary, and even less familiarity with among the English captains, Bedford sounded trumpets and ordered the whole fleet to attack en masse.

Before the favourable wind, the English ships raced towards the larger and more numerous French squadrons and although they suffered severely in the early stages of their attack from the enemy's artillery, cannon and ballistae, the ships which got through the barrage were soon locked together with their nearest opponent, their archers shooting down the Genoese and Navarene artillerymen, and their men-at-arms clambering aboard the enemy and settling matters hand-to-hand. With many of the French ships being lashed together to block the passage up-river, it was a simple matter for the boarders to carry the conflict from ship to ship and after several hours of fighting four of the great Genoese carracks had been taken and the rest had turned away from the battle. With the defeat of their finest men-of-war, the heart went out of the French fleet and those ships, which had not been captured or sunk, turned south for the safety of Honfleur harbour.

Bedford was among the many English wounded and he, with those others hurt in the fighting, returned to Southampton, taking a portion of the fleet and their four great prizes with him. The Earl of Hungerford assumed command of the expeditionary force and led the rest of the vessels with their priceless supplies into Harfleur harbour the following day, amidst general rejoicing. Similar expressions of joy appeared in England when Bedford brought news of his victory to the King, and Henry, with Emperor Sigismund, went immediately to Canterbury Cathedral where Te Deum was sung by a vast congregation.

Six years later, almost to the day, Harry of Monmouth, worn out by continual campaigning and a victim of the dysentery which continually plagued his army, died at Bois-de-Vincennes, shortly after his 35th birthday. With him, as he departed this life, were his brother, John of Bedford, who would take up Henry's mantle as Protector of his nephew's inheritance, and his uncle, Thomas Beaufort, now Duke of Exeter, who had himself but four more years left of life. He followed the King and nephew he had served so faithfully and signally on Old Year's Night 1426, at East Greenwich in Kent and was interred in the Abbey at Bury St Edmunds in Suffolk. His only child, a son named Henry for his brother, his half-brother and his King, had predeceased him; the Beaufort line through Thomas, Earl of Dorset, victor of Valmont, was extinguished.

CHAPTER FOUR

The Man of Means

Katherine Swynford's second son, Henry Beaufort, was, in the great English tradition of junior siblings, "destined for the Church". He made no difficulties over this early direction of his life's course and his clerical career soon flourished under his cousin, Richard II. He was Dean of Wells and Chancellor of Oxford University by 1397 at 24 years of age and, in the year following, was inducted as Bishop of Lincoln. In this capacity, he accompanied Richard on the disastrous expedition to Ireland, acting as companion to his nephew, the young Harry of Monmouth, whom he had come to know well during his time at Oxford. The future Henry V was included among the royal hostages in Richard's train, but was not required to pay the price of his father's treason, while Henry Beaufort switched easily to the cause of his half-brother, now King Henry IV, after returning to England.

He had the sad task of saying the Requiem Mass for his mother in May 1403, prior to her interment in his cathedral and, in the same year, the King made him Chancellor of England. Twelve months later he was translated to one of the richest sees in the English Church, that of Winchester, and the vast income from the manors of the Bishopric, together with Beaufort's shrewd investment in wool production and exporting would soon make and keep him one of the wealthiest Lords in the realm. At thirty years of age, Henry Beaufort was a made-man.

Beaufort and his brothers continued to work closely with the Prince of Wales and this brought them steadily into political conflict with the Prince's brother Thomas, Duke of Clarence, and his chief ally Thomas Fitzalan, Archbishop of Canterbury. For several years, the Beaufort alliance with the Prince steadily prospered, until, following the death of John Beaufort in 1410, Prince Henry, in addition to his duties as Constable of the Cinque Ports, was required to take on Beaufort's former office as Captain of Calais. At the January Parliament in that year, a new royal Council was formed, Thomas Fitzalan resigned the Chancellorship to Thomas Beaufort, and Henry

**Effigy of Cardinal Henry Beaufort,
Winchester Cathedral.**

(G. Wheeler)

Beaufort, Bishop of Winchester was the principal of only three clerics named to the new advisory body.

The Archbishop, however, was not yet a spent force and, following Winchester's faux pas in prematurely suggesting Henry's abdication on grounds of ill health, the King restored Fitzalan to the Chancellor's Office in the November of 1411 and simultaneously made Clarence leader of the Council. Prince Henry and the two Beauforts were "thanked for their services to King and country" and it was clear that Thomas of Clarence would be designated leader of the impending expedition to France.

Time for Prince Hal and his Beaufort uncles to wait for another turn of History's wheel, which came with the death of Henry IV and the crowning of his eldest son on April 9th, 1413. By the early summer of the year, King Henry had determined on an expedition to France and was secretly raising loans with which to lay in stocks of war materiel. His uncle Henry was an important donor to the fund with, amongst others, Dick Whittington. The Bishop's initial contribution amounted to 4,000 marks and his total lending to the King throughout his reign reached a figure of more than £35,000, indicative of the enormous wealth amassed by the Bishop of Winchester and its application in furthering the cause of the Lancastrian King, with which the aggrandisement of the House of Beaufort was ever more-closely linked.

Starting almost immediately after Henry's Coronation, Beaufort made himself leader of the new King's supportive faction in Parliament and, reciprocating, Henry restored his uncle to the Chancellorship. In the November Assembly of 1414, he reported that the King's mind was set on recovering his French inheritance. A year later, verifying his earlier statement, he was extolling Henry's victory at Agincourt and immediately after that he was demanding further financial support for the war-effort on a lavish scale which, naturally, was readily forthcoming. The alliance between Henry and his uncle worked smoothly and effectively until, quite suddenly, and strangely foreshadowing similar events a century later, a rift appeared in this ideal relationship.

A newly elected Pope, Martin V, was keen to restore the Papal authority in England, which had been much diminished during the latter half of the 14th century. His selected tool for this purpose was the prime politician amongst English churchmen, Henry Beaufort, Bishop of Winchester, whom Martin would designate Cardinal Legate to his English flock. Henry V, determined to maintain full control over church appointments within his realm, would have none of it and made clear to Beaufort that acceptance of the red hat would entail forfeiture of his wealth, his lands and his Bishopric, which could only mean, at best, penniless exile in the Curia. In the autumn of 1418, Henry Beaufort made his choice; he would forego the honour and continue as his nephew's strongest supporter, in earnest of which he made an immediate further loan of £22,000 to Henry's war chest.

Four years later, Henry V was dead and the Bishop of Winchester, soon to wear the long-coveted red hat, came fully into his own. He had financed a great deal of Henry's expenditure, over and above the generous grants from successive Parliaments, and the interest charges on his loans had become a considerable burden on the country's Exchequer. But, England's legislators tended to look less kindly on the financial demands of a Council of Regency on behalf of an infant King, than they had on those of his royal father, and the largesse of the Bishop of Winchester was even more essential to the upkeep of the court and the financing of the war than it had been in the reign of Henry V. In the first ten years of Henry VI's possession of the English throne, Henry Beaufort loaned his King and country more than £45,000, making him the pre-eminent power in the land – with one fly in his jar of ointment. The complication was called Humphrey, Duke of Gloucester, youngest brother of Henry V.

John of Bedford, Humphrey's elder brother, was Lord Protector and the undoubted ruler, in his nephew's behalf, of England and France. Unhappily, the war with the French continued and required Bedford's constant, personal attention, leaving England to the immediate control of the royal Council and Parliament. Duke Humphrey was named as Bedford's deputy while his older brother was out of the country, which made a serious conflict of interest between Gloucester and Cardinal Beaufort inevitable, and sooner rather than later.

The first open clash came at the end of October 1425, when Gloucester alerted the City Fathers to an impending coup by Henry Beaufort, which involved an armed incursion by the Cardinal's retainers, who were to take-over the Tower and win custody of the boy-King from his palace at Eltham.

The seizure of power was thwarted by Gloucester's warning and the prompt action of the Lord Mayor and Aldermen, who brought the people of London on to the streets in their thousands to defend the entry from the Southwark side of the bridge. For some hours the two sides glared in mutual antipathy from opposite sides of the crossing until peace was restored through the joint intermediacy of Archbishop Chichele and Prince Peter of Portugal, a grandson of John of Gaunt and thereby nephew to Beaufort and cousin to Gloucester.

Following Beaufort's discomfiture, Gloucester seized the opportunity to take closer control of the King, who was brought into the safety of London's walls on November 5th. On the same day, the Council agreed to loan Gloucester 5,000 marks for ten years, funds which the Duke needed to finance an expedition in support of his wife, Jacqueline of Hainault's territorial claims against England's chief ally, the Duke of Burgundy. The expedition was a dismal failure but its activities during the two months of its existence harmed relations between England and Burgundy and, following a worried message from Henry Beaufort to Bedford, the Lord Protector returned home to resolve the problem.

After despatch of deputations to the parties concerned, the formation of royal commissions, and on to, and through, declarations in Council and in Parliament, all of which occupied much of the following year, Humphrey of Gloucester eventually emerged victorious, formally recognised as Deputy Protector with appropriate powers whenever John of Bedford was out of the country. There had been a public reconciliation between the contenders with the usual vows of eternal friendship thereafter, but Beaufort apparently felt impelled, for whatever reason, to resign the Chancellorship, which he did on the 14th of March 1428 and then devoted himself, for the time being, to tasks given him by Martin V to restore Papal power in England. Then, in the summer of 1429, following further administrative delays, Pope Martin instructed Beaufort to preach a new Crusade against the Bohemian Hussites.

Unfortunately for the Holy Father and Henry, Cardinal Beaufort, the war in France was not going well. The siege of Orleans seemed to call unendingly for new quotas of manpower and the Council in April had heard a request from Bedford for another 200 lances and 12,000 archers to reinforce his army. In the event they were able to send only a hundred lances and 700 archers, which made Beaufort's official crusade allotment of 250 lances and 2,500 archers seem unduly generous. Worse was to come; the arrival on the military scene of Joan the Maid led to the raising of the siege and then, on June 18th to a shattering defeat for English troops, led by the redoubtable Talbot and Fastolf, at Patay. England's participation in the Bohemian Crusade was postponed and the Cardinal agreed to send the levies he had raised to relieve Bedford's manpower problems.

England's political problems were not eased by the continuing bitter rivalry between the Cardinal and Humphrey of Gloucester. The same Council which was unable to meet Bedford's request for troops, also heard a submission, engineered by Duke Humphrey, that Beaufort could not be a Cardinal of the Church of Rome and continue to be Bishop of Winchester, and was thereby disqualified from attending the Festival of St George as a prelate of the Garter. It was agreed that the position was "ambiguous" and, despite a plea to the King that he had attended the Festival of St George for 24 years past, the Council ruled it advisable that "for the present" Beaufort should abstain from attending this important ceremonial.

For two years following, Beaufort and his allies were able to neutralise Gloucester's continuing efforts to drive the Cardinal from the political stage, but, in November 1431, Humphrey arranged for the King's legal officers to petition that Henry Beaufort should be compelled to resign his see of Winchester. The Cardinal being in France at the time, it was decided to delay a formal hearing until his return and the suit was heard in May of the following year. The result was inconclusive, though Beaufort was again obliged to buy off his opponents, this time by returning the royal jewels he had held as security for one of his many loans to the Exchequer and making the crown a further loan of 10,000 marks.

The cost of the ongoing war with France was gradually ruining the English economy and growing French success in the field, sparked by the revelation of Joan's appearance on the scene, and increasing hopes of rapprochement between France and Burgundy, together made it inevitable that the two main protagonists would have to meet to discuss peace terms. The first significant moves occurred in January 1435, when Philip of Burgundy met the envoys of Charles of France at Nevers and a month later, a provisional peace treaty was signed. Both sides, however, recognised that nothing concrete could be settled without England's involvement and a tri-partite meeting was arranged at Arras in July. The chief English delegate to the conference was Henry Beaufort and Pope Martin appointed a Legate, Cardinal Alvergati, to oversee the negotiations.

The discussions were infinitely detailed and long drawn-out in consequence, but gradually some measure of agreement emerged with the French side making many concessions in terms of territory. At last, however, the main point of contention was reached, namely the requirement for the King of England to renounce his claim to the throne of France and on reaching this uncrossable abyss, the talks faltered and then collapsed. The English left Arras on September 6th; the state of war would continue. For Burgundy, on the other hand, the long struggle was effectively over and the alliance with England was discarded. In the same month, John of Bedford, worn out by incessant campaigning, sick at heart over the breakdown of negotiations to end the war, took to his bed and died. The last possible hope for continuation of English dominion in France was gone.

Surprisingly, for a time, the English cause flourished due largely to the exploits of Lord John Talbot who defeated superior French forces time and again. The recovery was also helped initially by Philip of Burgundy who, having made his own peace with Charles of France, urged his Flemish subjects to attack Calais, "the English dagger aimed at the heart of France" with predictable results. Calais was the one English possession which would never be surrendered and the mere threat of assault by the Flemings was enough to "summon up the blood" of all England. The attack was beaten off with heavy loss, including one of the first recorded losses of a ship of war to gunfire from on shore. This was a Flemish blockship which, together with three consorts which ran aground in the wrong place, constituted a most unsuccessful maritime support effort to the Flemish attacks.

This naval defeat, coming on top of fruitless assaults by their own troops on the stout walls of the port, was too much for the besiegers who broke camp and retreated towards Bruges. They were pursued as far as Gravelines by the victorious defenders, who returned to Calais in time to greet the arrival of Duke Humphrey with reinforcements. With his strong combined force, Humphrey now carried out a punitive raid through Flanders, burning Bailleul and Poperinghe and even threatening St Omer, following which demonstration of the continuing power of English arms, the Duke returned home to continue his leadership of the party supporting continuation of war with the French.

His chief opponent, as ever, was Cardinal Beaufort who, as became his Clerical calling, led the peace party, a role in which he was strongly supported – and later supplanted – by William de la Pole, Earl of Suffolk. Henry Beaufort's efforts culminated in a further peace conference between England and France in the high summer of 1439, which was held midway between Calais and Gravelines. The Cardinal led the English delegation, the French were led by the Duchess of Burgundy, her husband being overly mindful of a similar conference [with the French] twenty years before on the bridge of Montereau at which his father, Duke John had been assassinated. The meetings were lengthy and, with or without the ducal presence, were hopeless from the outset, since France's bottom line was the renunciation of the English claim to the crown of France. However, they did result in a three-year truce in the Calais area.

This left the French free to concentrate on the reclamation of their lands in Normandy and, later, in Gascony, where despite all Talbot's efforts, supplemented by those of a new commander in the north, Richard Plantagenet, Duke of York, the French continued, bit by bit, to reclaim their kingdom. Humphrey of Gloucester's standing in the English court had finally been broken in 1441, when his wife – and one-time mistress – Eleanor Cobham had been convicted of witchcraft and was condemned to life imprisonment. Gloucester himself was not involved in an alleged plot to bewitch the King, but his wife's disgrace left him under a permanent cloud and gave Henry Beaufort the freedom to secure command of a new English army to be sent to France, for his nephew, John Beaufort, Duke of Somerset, over the head of Richard of York.

The Cardinal's peace policy was exactly in tune with the thinking of Suffolk who, in 1444, negotiated secretly for a two-year truce with Charles VII which would be guaranteed by the betrothal of Margaret, daughter of the penniless pretender to the Kingdom of Jerusalem, Rene of Anjou, to King Henry VI of England. In the spring of 1445, a party of English nobles, led by Suffolk, went to France, where de la Pole stood proxy for his King and the marriage was duly celebrated. Humphrey of Gloucester briefly roused himself to point out that the truce merely gave Charles of France time and room to prepare for the final reconquest of his realm, but his voice no longer carried any weight in the King's Council.

In the following year, plans were developed to eliminate Gloucester's influence entirely by bringing charges of treason against him. The lead in the conspiracy against him was taken by Suffolk, who would bring the charge supported by his creatures, but the hidden hand of Cardinal Henry is not far to seek in the affair. Eventually, it was agreed that the Duke should be summoned to answer charges against him at Bury St Edmunds, where Suffolk's writ ran, and when Gloucester dutifully answered his King's warrant there on February 18th 1447, he was immediately arrested and, five days later, was found dead, without ever appearing to answer his accusers publicly.

His old enemy, Henry Beaufort, did not survive long to celebrate his ultimate triumph over the last son of Henry IV. Three weeks later, to the day, he died in his Palace at Winchester, some said stricken mad by remorse over the murder of Duke Humphrey. Be that as it may, he died with his work in the cause of peace seemingly well done. Within five years, English rule in France outside the Pale of Calais was a thing of the past, the War of a Hundred Years was ended, but England itself was about to enter on a period of bitter civil strife, which would last for 30 years. This internecine war would destroy half of England's peerage, including most of the House of Beaufort, and end the three-century rule of the Plantagenets. And, at its conclusion, it would usher in the new Renaissance which ended the Medieval age, and see the Beaufort bastard sprig triumph finally, through their heirs, the Tudors.

Signature of Cardinal Henry Beaufort

(G. Wheeler)

CHAPTER FIVE

The Matriarch

The only female child of John of Gaunt and Katherine Swynford was born in 1379 and christened Joan. She was married young to Robert, Baron Ferrers of Wemm and, in early proof of her subsequent amazing fertility, had borne him two girl children, Elizabeth and Mary, by the end of 1394. Two years later, Robert was dead and, by her second marriage to Ralph Neville, Lord of Middleham and Raby, later Earl of Westmorland, she would produce 14 more children, the first-born of whom was Richard, subsequently, by marriage, Earl of Salisbury and father of another Richard Neville, better known to later historians as Warwick the Kingmaker.

Ralph Neville's first marriage was to Margaret, daughter of Hugh, Earl of Stafford and produced nine children, a total which would undoubtedly have been greater had Margaret not died, still in her early thirties, on June 9th, 1396. The policy of successive Lords of Raby for nearly two hundred years had been to extend their wealth through arranged marriages with heiresses of landed families and this had proved sufficiently productive to make them the wealthiest and most powerful family in the north of England by the end of the 14th century. On February 3rd 1397, seven months after the death of his first wife, Ralph Neville set a capstone on the history of familial achievement in the marital field by marrying a granddaughter of one of the great Kings of England, Joan Beaufort, legitimised daughter of John of Gaunt, Duke of Lancaster. From now on, the blood royal would flow through the veins of Ralph Neville's descendants and his eminence in the land was further recognised when, at 34 years of age, he was raised to the dignity of Earl of Westmorland.

Such advancement of Earl Ralph's fortune and prospects could only have come about with the foreknowledge and encouragement of Richard II, indeed, the Earldom was conferred amongst similar ennoblements of Bolingbroke, Mowbray and Holland, all intended to bind key nobles to Richard's cause. However, two year's later, when Bolingbroke returned from exile in France to demand first his Duchy and then the throne itself, his half-sister's husband, Ralph of Westmorland, with 3,000 men, marched at his side, not at Richard's. And, for the first 25 years of Lancastrian rule, the Neville fortunes continued to wax strong through Ralph's loyal adherence to the usurping branch of the House of Plantagenet.

On October 21st 1425, Ralph died at the mature age of 62 and was buried in the church he had founded at Staindrop, close to his ancestral home of Raby Castle. His eldest son, John, had predeceased him and the title of Westmorland passed to John's son, another Ralph, but with it went only the "pye's nest" of Brancepeth and a handful of other manors in Durham. It was to his royal Countess Joan that the old Earl left the bulk of his wide, rich estates in north Yorkshire and County Durham with the great Keeps at Raby and Penrith, Middleham and Sheriff Hutton. It was a rare error of judgement on Ralph's part and one which would sunder his children from a united family into two separate, feuding halves whose rivalry contributed in large measure to the impending civil war in England.

Immediately, however, Joan, now Dowager Countess of Westmorland, having persuaded her uxorious Lord to endow her with the vast bulk of his considerable wealth, showed she had no intention of correcting the apparent injustice to her step-children. What was now hers she would hold, and by force of arms if necessary. This determination was backed fully by her eldest son Richard, soon to become Earl of Salisbury in right of his wife, and the senior branch of the family received no redress. The young Ralph, when he came of age in 1429, immediately initiated legal proceedings to contest his effective disinheritance, but Joan, with her much greater wealth and wider connections, proved equal to this challenge and to successive suits which occupied much of the last ten years of her life. As her mother had repelled the attempted depredations of the citizens of Lincoln on her "Rights", so Joan Beaufort fended off the attempts of her stepchildren to recover that which her husband had allotted to her.

Similarly, when the Westmorland faction, despairing of legal restoration of their rights, took up arms in their own cause, their lack of funds and, therefore, of retainers meant their numbers were always less than those Salisbury could command and their incursions were repelled, with loss and damage to persons and property of both sides and of neither. These regular outbreaks of violence eventually attracted the attention of the Royal Council

Effigy of Joan Beaufort, Countess of Westmorland.

(Detail from a drawing by Charles A. Stothard)

(G. Wheeler)

through complaints from innocent bystanders of "the slaughter and destruction of the King's lieges ... which things are greatly against the weal and peace of this Royaume of England". This complaint led to a patched-up peace between the warring parties, but it was not until after the Countess Joan had died that a more durable armistice was possible.

In 1443, eighteen years after old Ralph had split his own family in two, Richard Neville, Earl of Salisbury and his nephew Ralph, second Earl of Westmorland, made an accord whereby Salisbury kept the rich Yorkshire estates willed to him by his mother and Ralph recovered the ancient family seat of Raby and all the surrounding lands his lovesick grandfather had unnecessarily heaped upon his royal wife. The healing of the breach was, unhappily for both branches, more apparent than real. Ralph, second Earl of Westmorland, with his brothers John and Thomas, harboured grudges throughout their lifetimes against the wealthier, nobler Middleham Nevilles and, when the new family affiliations of the junior branch took them into the Yorkist camp in the conflict soon now to come, their half-brethren would ever be found in the opposing ranks and many on both sides would die as a result. Envy grown from injustice is a bitter herb.

Three years before the shallow settlement, on November 13th 1440, Joan Neville, nee Beaufort, the only daughter of Katherine Swynford acknowledged by John of Gaunt, had died and her body was taken to lie, not beside Earl Ralph, her doting husband, but to be interred by her mother's great tomb in Lincoln Cathedral. She left behind four daughters, three of whom would become Duchesses whose husbands and sons would fight and die on opposite sides in the oncoming war. Her eldest son would be lynched in the aftermath of a battle which should never have been fought and in which her step-grandson, John Neville, fought on the other side. And two of her grandsons would become Kings of England and lead armies into battles which very nearly exterminated the proud bloodline of Beaufort, stemming from the would-be King, John of Gaunt, Duke of Lancaster. Thankfully, neither the Lady Joan, nor her immediate descendants, could have envisioned the cruel paths, which Destiny had in store for them.

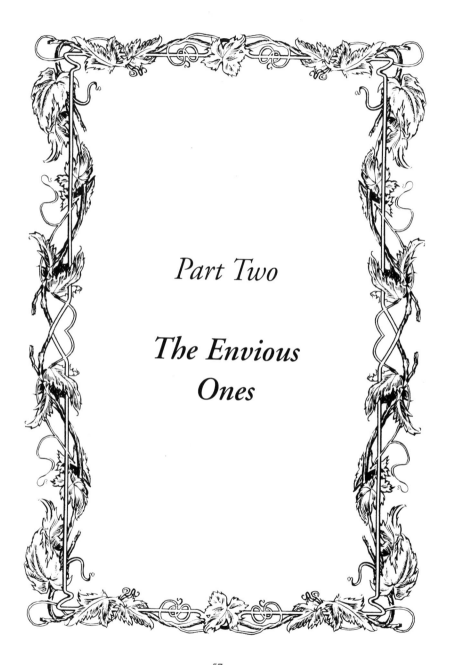

Part Two

The Envious Ones

Effigy of John Beaufort, 1st Duke of Somerset and his wife, Margaret Beauchamp, parents of Margaret Beaufort. Wimborne Minster

(G. Wheeler)

CHAPTER SIX

The Peculator

In the August of 1443, the year in which Earl Ralph made his counterfeit peace with Richard of Salisbury, the main French army under Dunois, the Bastard of Orleans, broke the English siege of Dieppe by capturing a large bastille built there by Lord Talbot to house the thousand or so troops he left to blockade the port. The entire force was made prisoner and this reverse triggered renewed interest in England in the prospect of a more aggressive campaign being waged against the Dauphin. The immediate result was the despatch of a new army, 7,000 strong, to secure English possessions in Gascony and, if possible, to extend them. Command of the force was given to John Beaufort, first Duke of Somerset and eldest nephew of Cardinal Beaufort whose faction was in full control of the English political scene.

The biased decision to send Beaufort was, effectively, a slight on Richard, Duke of York, who held the title of King's Lieutenant in France and, with Talbot, could well have used the large force sent over with Somerset to better effect in Normandy. Somerset had no experience in war. As a young man, around eighteen years of age, he had marched with the army of the disorganised Thomas, Duke of Clarence, brother to Henry V, to Baugé on March 22nd 1421 and been captured after that disastrous melée. John Beaufort spent the next seventeen years of his life in French captivity and was the last English prisoner of quality taken in that fight to be released.

Unfortunately for his dreams of building a belated martial reputation, and for the hopes of the men he led of quick fortunes to be made, he had equally little skill in seamanship. It may have been down to mal de mer, or poor navigation, or simply some wild scheme of his own, but whatever the reason, instead of making Bordeaux, he took the shorter crossing to Cherbourg in Normandy. From this port he marched south along the border between Maine and Brittany, eventually – with plunder in mind it has been alleged – he swung west into Brittany and captured the town of La Guerche which lies 25 miles south east of Rennes.

Whatever John Beaufort's purpose, his action was one of monumental folly, since Brittany had just signed a treaty of friendship with England and had not expected its ally's newest field commander to make his first objective one of their own townships. Fortunately, no lasting harm was done to Anglo/Breton relations and Somerset withdrew his army, "the duke of Brittany having given some sum of money to the duke of Somerset..." a few days later. For the next three months, the English army wandered aimlessly around the County of Maine neither meeting nor seeking French opponents and their enemy was quite happy to let this unending, pointless chevauchée continue until the English tired of it and went away again.

After a few weeks of nomadic inaction, Somerset received a deputation of his captains who asked if he would reveal to them his strategy. John Beaufort frowned and, pre-empting a much abler General who was asked the same question 370 years later, near a Belgian village called Waterloo, said "I do not divulge my secret to anyone. If even my own shirt knew my secret I should burn it". The episode was recorded for posterity by a French Bishop, Basin, who added the comment that Somerset's secret was buried so deep that even he probably did not know what it was. Be that as it may, the general and the army at last grew equally tired of eternal perambulation around an area where there was no prospect of hostilities arising, located 350 miles north of their original objective, and in January 1444, weary and disillusioned, the whole army returned to England.

As a prominent member of the ascendant Beaufort/Suffolk faction, Somerset was not prosecuted for gross neglect of duty amounting almost to treasonable inactivity. His pathetic adventure however had a two-fold effect on the politics of England and France seemingly out of all proportion to its ineffectual nature. First, the return of such a large, well-equipped army with its tail between its legs, having accomplished nothing other than causing offence to England's ally, was a body-blow to the country's morale which, however, did much to clarify the future policy of the ruling party. The war with France must be brought to an end and, to achieve this, a French bride should be sought for the young King Henry. Helpfully, the Duke of Orleans suggested that a niece of Charles VII would fit the bill admirably. The girl was beautiful and her blood-line impeccable, all of which compensated amply for the fact that she had no dowry as such. Her name was Margaret, daughter of Rene, Count of Anjou.

The second problem rising directly from the failed expedition was the waste of money entailed, and the affront the creation of this separate command had given to Richard of York. The Duke must have felt slighted by the difference in treatment of himself and Somerset. On the one hand, a powerful, new army, fully provided with arms, equipment and funds, which was uselessly shuffled around northern France for four months and then re-embarked for home and not a word of blame or reproach for its so-called commander. For him, a constant struggle to provide the fresh men and arms John Talbot desperately needed to continue the war and a continual shortage of funds to pay his men and his suppliers.

York had been in France as King's Lieutenant for three of a five years engagement, for which he was guaranteed £20,000 per year and in 1446, two years after Somerset's debacle, he was still trying to get his money from the Treasury for the final period of his tour of duty. He was owed £18,666 13s 4d for the fourth year and the whole £20,000 for the fifth, a total roughly equivalent to £70 million in current terms. It was fortunate for York – and for England – that the Duke was the wealthiest man in the country since no other lord could or would have carried such a burden. York was eventually relieved, though probably not happy, to settle for £26,000 paid the year after his commission expired.

John Beaufort spent little time reflecting on the dishonour he had brought on his name and country, or the growing enmity between Lancaster and York resulting largely from his own poor showing as a general in the field. His death is recorded as occurring on May 27th 1444, some three months after his inglorious return from France. There were rumours of diversion of funds provided for his war-chest to his own pockets and indications of first a possible, then increasingly probable, summons to answer for such peculation grew in strength. Whatever the real substance of such reports, they may have led on to suicide. Or perhaps John Beaufort at last decided to redeem something of his and his family's honour and, literally, fell on his sword.

However it came about, it made a widow for a second time of Margaret Beauchamp, who had been his wife for little more than four years and rendered fatherless their only child, an infant girl whose first birthday celebration was marred by her father's demise four days previously. The child was called Margaret after her mother, and she carried within her tiny body the seed which would ultimately destroy the Plantagenet Dynasty forever. She would be John Beaufort's final, catastrophic legacy to his land, to his countrymen, and to his own familial House.

Garter Stall Plate of John Beaufort, 1st Duke of Somerset.

(G. Wheeler)

CHAPTER SEVEN

The Queen's Man

In addition to his widow and only child, John Beaufort left behind two sisters. The younger, Margaret, married Thomas Courtenay, 5th Earl of Devon and by him produced five children, including the 6th Earl, named Thomas for his father, who would die at Towton fighting for Lancaster. Joan, the elder girl, married James I of Scotland on February 2nd 1423, had eight children by him and a further three subsequently by Sir James Stewart. She died a year after her eldest brother, and her sister Margaret, in the November of 1449. John also had two brothers, Thomas, Earl of the French county of Perche, who died young and left no issue, and Edmund, who succeeded to the Somerset earldom on his brother's death and acceded to the dukedom four years later. To England's dire cost, Edmund Beaufort's career would follow that of his brother in one further particular.

By the time of the near-simultaneous deaths of Humphrey of Gloucester and Henry, Cardinal Beaufort, in the early spring of 1447, William de la Pole, shortly to become Duke of Suffolk, had assumed the leadership of the Court Party. The truce negotiated at Tours in 1444 by Suffolk had been twice extended and now de la Pole redoubled his efforts to achieve a permanent settlement of hostilities with the French, almost regardless of cost. A key move in his strategy was the early removal of Richard of York as the English commander in France, which he achieved by the simple device of making him Viceroy in Ireland. In York's place as commander in France, Suffolk sent Edmund Beaufort, now Duke of Somerset, an appointment which sounded the final death-knell for English rule in France, as the second Duke would prove himself more inept in military affairs even than his older brother.

At the beginning of 1449, England still held most of Normandy and Gascony. In the northern dukedom, England's forces were split into garrisons for the main fortified towns, there was no effective field army to counter the impressive French host Charles VII had assembled, outnumbering the English by two to one and being particularly well-equipped with siege artillery. The extended truce was still holding, but Charles was becoming increasingly impatient with the delaying tactics employed by Suffolk to avoid handing over the capital of Maine, Le Mans. When, as a further distraction, Suffolk, through Edmund Beaufort, ordered a raid on Brittany's border towns, notably Fougères, this was the last straw for the King of France, who ordered his men into Normandy, with the armed support of the Duke of Brittany.

The French, thanks to the small size and wide separation of England's garrisons, were able to follow a strategy of piece-meal attacks and, after a number of minor triumphs, took Rouen in October. Somerset himself had commanded in the capital and was allowed to withdraw on terms, after providing hostages, including the great John Talbot. Edmund Beaufort meantime, pursued his warlike way to Caen and there settled to await further developments. These came quickly. Harfleur, the port whence Monmouth Harry had commenced his conquest of France, fell in December and in January, 1450, its sister port across the estuary, Honfleur, also became French territory once more.

These losses raised alarm in England where Suffolk scraped a small relieving force of 2,500 men together and sent it to Cherbourg under an experienced soldier, Sir Thomas Kyriel, who had orders to march immediately to the relief of Bayeux. Instead, Kyriel waited for reinforcement from Somerset and then attacked Valognes, which he took on April 10th. Afterwards, he moved on towards Bayeux, but was caught between two French columns on April 15th near the village of Formigny and the last English army in Normandy was destroyed in detail. Kyriel was taken prisoner and Charles of France ordered his army to retake the remaining towns in Normandy. Caen was invested in June and Somerset, who had his wife and children with him, again made terms, after three weeks intensive bombardment by the French artillery. A decisive factor may have been the cannon ball which penetrated the Somersets' nursery, narrowly missing the Duchess. Edmund Beaufort was offered safe conduct and free passage to England, but preferred instead to take his laissez-passer to Calais and wait on developments there.

His decision was, no doubt, strongly influenced by recent events in the home country. There, at the beginning of February, William de la Pole had been summoned to answer accusations of conspiring with the French to invade England. The King, urged on by his French Queen, had prevaricated

64

but on March 9th, the Commons brought a new Bill, charging the Duke with maladministration, embezzlement and misappropriation of taxes. Suffolk denied all the accusations and while Henry found the treason charges not proven, he sentenced the Duke to banishment overseas for five years on the second Bill. Suffolk was given time to clear up his affairs and eventually sailed for France on the last day of April. His vessel was intercepted in the Dover Straits and Suffolk paid the full penalty for his shortcomings, being beheaded by a common seaman wielding, according to report, "a rusty sword". His body was thrown on to the beach at Dover where it lay until King Henry ordered its burial at Wingfield.

Suffolk's murder acted as a signal for outbreaks of violence across England. On June 29th, the Bishop of Salisbury, a close friend of Suffolk who spent more time at court than in his see, was dragged from the altar at Edington Church, where he was saying mass, and brutally hacked to death by local parishioners. He was particularly hated by the Commons as the priest who had formalised the marriage between Henry VI and Margaret of Anjou when she arrived in England. On the day of his demise, a Kentish rebel army, reported at more than 40,000 men, was moving towards their appointed rendezvous at Blackheath by Greenwich. They were led by an Irishman called Jack Cade, who, as a nom de guerre, called himself John Mortimer, claiming relationship with the Plantagenet House of York.

Cade had already met and defeated at Sevenoaks, a weak force led by Sir Humphrey and William Stafford, who had been sent by the King to disperse the rebels. Both leaders of the loyal force were killed and the surviving officers were obliged to flee for their lives, among them Richard Woodville, Lord Rivers. Cade's army moved to Southwark on July 2nd and the following day fought their way into the city across the draught bridge. In their manifesto, the rebels claimed – with some justice at least – that the King's Council had lost his Law and his goods; that the common people were destroyed; the sea was lost; France was lost and that the King could not pay for his meat and drink and owed more than any King of England ought. All these faults were laid at the door of the traitors about the King who daily asked him for the goods and moneys which should rightly have gone to him.

Particularly named among the "traitors" was William Cromer, Sheriff of Kent, together with his father-in-law, James Fiennes, Lord Saye and Sele. Both gentlemen were in the Tower for safety's sake, but the loyal troops now arriving in London were unwilling to defend them. The rebel army got wind of this and seized the fortress, whence they dragged Cromer and Saye and summarily executed them. Their heads were displayed together on poles on London Bridge. The rebellion was descending into anarchy and when Cade broke open the King's Bench and the Marshalsea prisons, freeing the criminal inmates, the populace of London had had enough. Under the leadership of Thomas, Lord Scales, the citizens and the loyal army turned on the men from Kent and drove them out of the city. London Bridge was burned down by the rebels to protect their retreat from the capital and they made camp on the south bank of the Thames to await further developments.

The following day, John Stafford, Archbishop of Canterbury and William Waynflete, Bishop of Winchester, met with Cade and his captains and, in exchange for a Charter granting all their demands and pardoning them for rebellion, the men from Kent broke camp and started for their homes. Once the rebel host had dissolved, Cade was proclaimed traitor and outlaw with a price of 1,000 marks on his head and on July 12th, he was caught in hiding in the Sussex weald by a gentleman, Sir Alexander Iden, and killed. By a strange twist of fate, Iden went on to marry Cromer's widow, Saye's daughter, presumably as a bonus for wreaking vengeance on her beloved parent's murderer.

Meanwhile in Normandy, the French army had moved on to Falaise and thence to the last target, Cherbourg, which surrendered on August 11th 1450. English dominance in northern France was finally over. In the same month, Richard of York returned to England from Ireland and Edmund Beaufort judged it politic to follow him there in September, his presence being requested urgently by Queen Margaret and the King's Council.

One year later, French troops were in the streets of Bordeaux. Answering the pleas of the citizens of this "English" port, a small expeditionary force under Talbot, now Earl of Shrewsbury, landed in Gascony in October 1452 and, for a few months, the ancient rule of England was reinstalled throughout much of the County. On the 17th of July 1453, however, John Talbot led his last attack, a charge intended to break the French siege of Castillon, and was killed. For the first time in close on 300 years, with the sole exception of Calais and its surrounding Pale, the King of France ruled the whole of his land in fact as well as in name. From England's coat, one half was indeed stripped away.

And in England, the cast was assembling, the stage being set for thirty years of Civil War through which England would pay a heavy price for the ambition of their late King, his marriage with the daughter of a madman, and the vaunting pride of the brood raised by the bastards of John of Gaunt and Katherine Swynford.

On his return from France, Edmund Beaufort, Duke of Somerset, was made Constable of England and became the Queen's chief ally in the looming political battles between the rival royal houses of York and Lancaster that were to follow. For three years prior to the ending of the wars with France, Parliament tried, vainly, to pass legislation which would restore much of the revenue from the King's estates to his own use. Unfortunately, the magnates who enjoyed these incomes were unwilling to forego this wealth and Henry, who had weakly donated the benefits under the influence of his wife and her favourites, was still dominated by his court and Queen and agreed to amendments and modifying clauses which effectively negated reforms put forward by the Commons. The result, as written in Cade's Manifesto, was that the King was made penniless to the gain of venal nobles and high Churchmen.

In the Parliament of 1451, an apprentice in law, Thomas Yonge, Member for Bristol, moved that in the continuing absence of royal issue, there should be common agreement on who should be heir apparent and Yonge's nomination for the position was Richard, Duke of York. The proposal was approved by the Commons and Yonge was nominated to present it to the Lords and Monarch, which he duly did. For this temerity, he was committed to the Tower on June 11th. Whether or not York had "encouraged" Yonge to put forward his proposal, he made little progress with other efforts to restore good governance to the land. So long as King and Council were dominated by the Queen and Somerset, all efforts to improve matters were bound to fail.

In January 1452, York rode from his stronghold at Ludlow, accompanied by the Earl of Devon and Lord Cobham and a large contingent of fighting-men to seek redress of his grievances against Edmund Beaufort and his party, and to protest his loyalty to Henry VI. The King with an equally powerful force commanded by Somerset and Buckingham set out to meet him but the two armies missed each other and York made for London. He was denied access to the city and crossed the Thames at Kingston, making camp at Dartford in Kent. The King passed through London and the two bodies met at Blackheath, where, thanks to the intercession of the Bishops of Winchester and Ely, and the Earls of Salisbury and Warwick, hostilities were avoided on condition that Somerset was sent to the Tower till he should be called to answer the charges York had made against him.

Satisfied, York sent his army away, but, on answering a summons to the King's tent found Somerset still there, leading the attendance on Henry, and himself then obliged to ride into London, without his sword and between the two Bishops. As part of a celebratory mass at St Paul's, York was required to swear loyalty to the King on the Holy Sacrament and might himself have ended in the Tower had reports not arrived that the young Earl of March was coming to London at the head of 11,000 men to ensure his father's safety. York was freed to return to Ludlow, but he left London with his petitions unanswered and with his rival, Somerset, seemingly established more firmly even than before as the power behind the throne. York took advantage of a general pardon issued by the King on April 7th, 1452, and the King visited Ludlow in August during a royal progress, but York was not summoned to meetings of the Council during the rest of the year.

A Parliament was summoned at Reading in March, 1453 which annulled reforming measures enacted under the pressures of Cade's rebellion and attainted Sir William Oldhall, Speaker of the previous Parliament, for supporting Cade. Oldhall was man of substance. who had already been publicly branded a thief by Somerset and Jasper Tudor, Earl of Pembroke and half-brother to the King, but whose chief crime was to be Chamberlain to Richard, Duke of York. Oldhall was outlawed and attainted and his lands were divided between his accusers, the lions' share going to Edmund Beaufort and Tudor. And, in the same Parliament, special provision was made for a force of archers 13,000 strong to be recruited for the King's service, for a period of six months, purpose unspecified.

On the 17th of July, John Talbot lost his life at Castillon, England lost its last remaining possession in France outside the Pale of Calais and, three weeks later and possibly under the stress caused by these events, Henry VI became insane. His condition was concealed from the public for some time but, on October 13th, St Edward's Day, Margaret of Anjou bore a son, making essential the summoning of a Great Council to mark the birth of a Lancastrian heir to the crown. Initially, Somerset hoped to exclude York from the meeting but found this impossible and so York was "instructed to attend". For several months, Somerset and the Queen attempted to rule via the Council, and then Margaret, in January 1454, demanded that the Lords should place the government of the realm within her hands, until the King recovered his senses. Unfortunately for Margaret, and for Edmund Beaufort, this was a step too far even for their accommodating Council and, with disorder growing daily throughout the country, in the March of 1454, Richard Plantagenet, Duke of York was made Protector of England.

The new Protector moved quickly to reinforce his grip on the governance of the land, ending public disorder in the southwest and in the north of England, taking over the Captaincy of Calais from Somerset, who for his own safety, was lodged in the Tower, and having his previous appointment as Governor of Ireland confirmed by Council. Unhappily for the Duke of York and for the well-being of the Kingdom, Henry recovered his wits, appropriately perhaps for so Christian a ruler, on Christmas Day 1454. He declared himself "in charity with all the world and so he would his lords were".

The King's high hopes were not, in the event, justified. Somerset was quickly released from the Tower and the court party again assumed the rule of the Kingdom, losing no time in reversing all the policies York had initiated. In the early spring of the year, a girl of twelve who, as only daughter of the late John, first Duke of Somerset, was titular head of the Beaufort family, married the King's half-brother, Edmund, Earl of Richmond. Her name was Margaret and she had been a ward of Richmond for two years prior to the wedding. The link between the throne and the Beauforts was further strengthened by the union, and it was clear that, in the event of the King's health again deteriorating, or anything untoward happening to Edward his infant son, the Beauforts would have a major role in any reshaping of the government of England.

Shortly after the wedding ceremony, Edmund Beaufort and Queen Margaret persuaded the King to summon a meeting of the Great Council to be held at Leicester at the end of May. The Duke of York was not required to attend and can have been in little doubt as to what was intended for him. After his Protectorate had ended, Richard Plantagenet had gone north to his keep at Sandal to await developments and when intelligence of the Council summons reached him, he realised that the threat to his own, and his family's safety was become overwhelming. Therefore, he summoned Salisbury and Warwick, with Sir Robert Ogle, the battle-hardened Constable of Norham Castle, and sundry other gentlemen-retainers to join him at Wakefield, armed and ready to march south.

The Duke of Somerset was in no great hurry to move from London to the appointed meeting place, but was able to pass the time usefully in talks with Humphrey Stafford, Duke of Buckingham; Lord Thomas Clifford; Harry Percy, Earl of Northumberland; the handsome fop James Butler, Lord Treasurer and Earl of Wiltshire and Ormonde, and the former Speaker of the House of Commons, Thomas Thorpe, an old enemy of York and one well-versed in "arranging" Council agendas. Then, on May 20th news arrived that a strong army led by York and his Neville allies had set off from Yorkshire, presumably to meet with the King at Leicester and the time for discussion was over.

Somerset and his allies quickly mustered their men and, on the morning of May 21st, marched north up the Edgeware road, reaching Watford where they rested for the night. Edmund Beaufort, though not expecting to meet the northern men until he was well north of the capital, had taken the precaution of sending scouts forward and they brought back news that York and the Earls were camped at Ware just 20 miles to the northeast. The King's army broke camp in the early hours of the morning of May 22nd and marched at breakneck speed to St Albans, the traditional gateway to London. York's own scouts had been disturbed by Somerset's prickers and, guessing that the King must be moving towards Leicester with a substantial force, the Duke broke camp and marched directly towards St Albans, whence Watling Street headed due northeast towards the town appointed as the Council's meeting place.

Passing south of Hatfield, the Yorkist army, 3,000 strong, marched up Shropshire Lane towards the old Tonman Ditch which defended St Alban's eastern approaches, only to find that the bars – great tree-trunks which blocked the ditch-crossings – had been swung across their path preventing further advance. Deploying to the left, Salisbury found that the approach by

Sopwell Lane had been similarly stopped and, behind both barriers, the early sun glinted on spear points and helmets. Edmund Beaufort awaited his old antagonist's attack which he would ensure should be the last meeting between Somerset and York. Tired by their forced marching and broken sleep, both armies settled either side of the ditch to rest, eat, and await developments.

The Yorkist leaders were also awaiting a response from the King to a letter sent by Richard Plantagenet setting out his grievances against Somerset and his allies and when trumpets sounded a parley and they saw the Duke of Buckingham emerging from behind the barrier across Shropshire Lane, they anticipated that he would be bringing the royal response to their pleas for redress. Unfortunately, York's letter had been diplomatically suppressed by Somerset and all that Buckingham brought was a direct command from King Henry to disband their forces and to yield themselves to his mercy, lest they be attainted as rebels against their undoubted liege-lord.

York, remembering events three years earlier under very similar circumstances, simply replied that while they remained the King's loyal subjects, they were concerned at the evil advice he was given by the Lords closest to him and respectfully requested that "such as we shall name" should be handed over to them. When Henry heard their response he cried, "I shall destroy these traitors, every mother's son and they shall be hanged, drawn and quartered". The time for talking was finally past and, with defiant shouts, the Yorkist columns advanced towards the log barriers, York leading his force up Shropshire Lane towards the town centre, where the Beaufort standard was flaunting in the noon sunlight, with Salisbury, his brother-in-law, on his left commanding the attack up Sopwell Lane. Neither assault made progress and to the taunts of their adversaries, the Yorkshire troops withdrew to regroup.

Meantime, between the two divisions, Richard Neville, 27 years old and Earl of Warwick, was awaiting his baptism in battle. With him was Robert Ogle, a master of the craft of war, which he had learned over years of fighting Scottish raiders from his keep at Norham, which towered over the well-named Hangman's Land and glowered across the River Tweed at any Scot foolish enough to dream of crossing the Border. Ogle noted that there was no apparent opposition mounted to the immediate front of their division, which counted near 1,200 men of which half were his own Border troopers. He suggested to Warwick that they should advance quietly through the fields, allotments and gardens to their front when the second assaults on the log

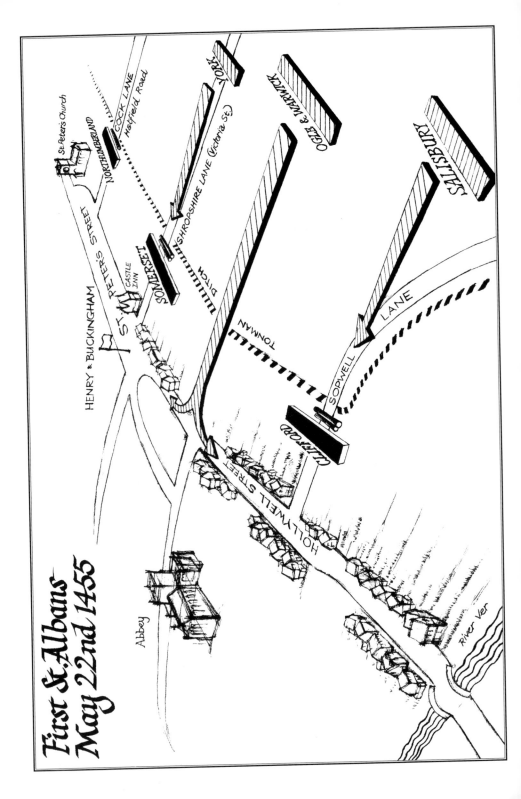

First St. Albans
May 22nd 1455

barriers began. With the Earl's agreement, their column moved quietly forward as soon as the uproar of battle recommenced and, finding no hindrance to their progress, quickened their pace until they came to the backs of houses, which faced on to the top of Holywell Hill. Wasting no time they broke through the walls, charged past the terrified tenants and out of the front doors into the main street beyond.

Here, and with great shouts of "A Warwick, A Warwick", they swung left and right and charged into the flank and rear of the forces blocking their main bodies' attacks, sweeping them aside and permitting York and Salisbury to bring their men into the action. The end was never in doubt and, within minutes, the royal army was reduced to shreds of fleeing men and horses clearing out of the town in any and every direction, so long as it was away from the invading Yorkist host. Among the escapers was James Butler, Earl of Wiltshire, who had played little part in the conflict through fear of spoiling his handsome features and Thomas Thorpe, ex-Speaker of the Commons. Taken captive – briefly – were the King and Buckingham, both slightly wounded by arrows, but his Grace apparently pleased to receive the apologies and loyal protestations from his erstwhile rebels. Less fortunate than either were Thomas, Lord Clifford, dead in the Sopwell Lane entrance he had defended so stubbornly, and Harry Percy, second Earl of Northumberland, who had taken little part in the fighting other than guarding Cock Lane. The slain body of Edmund Beaufort, Duke of Somerset and last surviving male of John of Gaunt's grandchildren was found on the steps of the Castle Inn.

Somerset was an inept military commander, overly proud of his royal descent, but with great personal charm when he cared to exercise it. Together with the Queen, he was a bad influence on Henry VI and planted many seeds, whose burgeoning would eventually contribute to the destruction of the House of Lancaster from which he sprang, and of the House of Plantagenet itself. Among these plantlets were his three sons and his five daughters, the youngest of whom was married to another of the St Albans dead, Humphrey, Earl of Stafford, by whom she had a boy-child, Henry, who, as the second Duke of Buckingham, would eventually carry the family tradition of treachery and pride of blood to new extremes of folly.

Among the wounded at St Albans was the young Henry Beaufort, Earl of Dorset, who had accompanied his father in the royal train. Still in his teens, Henry would follow his father as third Duke of Somerset and Richard Neville,

73

Earl of Warwick, took the young, new head of the House of Beaufort into his personal care till his wounds be healed. A conciliatory gesture entirely wasted on this proud, handsome scion of the descendants of John of Gaunt, who would show himself as feckless in war as any of his kin and as faithless to any bond which did not involve the advancement of his familial pride and status to its rightful place in the English hierarchy. Unhappily for the realm of England, he would figure large in the bloodiest years of all its history.

Memorial plaque in St Albans to Edmund Beaufort,
2nd Duke of Somerset

(G. Wheeler)

74

Part Three

The Warmakers

Henry VI

(Detail from the w.w.w.)

CHAPTER EIGHT

The General

The Yorkist victory at St Albans did nothing to resolve their political difficulties with the Queen's party at court, nor did the crude ramming of a Bill through the July Parliament, which laid the entire blame for the battle at the door of the late Edmund Beaufort, reconcile the Lords or the people to the Duke of York's cause. This was made evident by the activities of Thomas Courtenay, Earl of Devon, a firm adherent of Lancaster, who revived old quarrels with Lord Bonville and his supporters and started out on a campaign of raiding and rioting, which climaxed on October 23rd 1455 with the robbery and murder of Sir Nicholas Radford.

This was reported to the November Parliament and York was, rather grudgingly, appointed Protector of the realm with a particular remit to put down the disorder in the west. Unhappily for the Yorkist cause, the threat of firm counteraction alone was enough to quell the Courtenays and the grounds for York's appointment as defender of the Kingdom were immediately, and seriously, undermined. By the time Parliament reconvened on January 14th 1456, the Protector's position had been so weakened that even the feeble King Henry, urged on by his Queen and her chief ally, Henry Beaufort, felt able to intervene in the governance of his land and, late in February, appeared personally in the Parliament and removed York from his Office.

With the King firmly in her control once again, Queen Margaret moved the court out of London to Lancaster's traditional power-base in the northwest, where she worked assiduously and successfully to increase the strength of her party. In September, she moved the court to Coventry, where it stayed for most of the following twelve months enlisting support from the Midlands. Somerset moved to the family's lands in the southwest, where he started actively to recruit support for Lancaster's cause, as did young Henry Percy, soon to be confirmed as third Earl of Northumberland, from his Alnwick stronghold. Meantime, York had retired to his own keep in Ludlow where he could watch the Marches and the Midlands; Salisbury, from

Middleham, guarded the north and Warwick, now Captain of Calais, made an additional base in the French port, whence he could more easily observe the Channel and Kent.

In the absence of any strong authority in the capital, the London mob began to stir and attacks on foreigners and on the Inns of Court became commonplace. In October, Thomas Bourchier, Archbishop of Canterbury, who, as Chancellor, had tried to broker better relations between York and the court, was dismissed and replaced by William Waynflete, a member of the Queen's service, as was Lawrence Booth who took the Privy Seal. The trade in wool and cloth with Flanders was disrupted by French pirates whose depredations reached a peak in August 1457 when a strong fleet led by Pierre de Brézé, Seneschal of Normandy, attacked and sacked Sandwich, only seven miles from Canterbury. They killed the town's bailiffs, ministers and rectors of the church, and wealthier inhabitants in the process and then beat a successful retreat, taking a great booty with them.

England was clearly slipping towards civil war and, in the early spring of 1458, the peace-loving King Henry, with his Council, arranged a Grand Reconciliation ceremony, celebrating promises made by York, Salisbury and Warwick to pay an annual rent of £45 to the Abbey of St Albans, which would provide perpetual masses for the souls of those slain in the battle there. To mark the occasion, on Our Lady's Day in Lent, a formal procession led by the King and, in pairs, Henry Beaufort with Richard of York, Salisbury with James Butler, Earl of Wiltshire, and Warwick with the new Lord Clifford, walked together from the Bishop of London's Palace to St Paul's, where a solemn service of thanksgiving was sung for this new accord.

That this gratitude was somewhat premature was made clear in the following October, when Warwick was summoned to appear before the Council to answer for attacks his Calais fleet had made on ships owned by the Hanseatic League. He arrived in England in November and on the 8th was well-received by the King, chatting sociably with him about events in Picardy. The following day was a different story. Council had hardly convened when uproar broke out in the anterooms with much shouting for Warwick. When the Earl appeared, he found his retainers being attacked by Somerset's men, and he himself was quickly dragged into the brawl and barely escaped with his life, with two followers cutting his way down the water stairs and into a boat moored there. He returned to Calais, without waiting for further assassination attempts to materialize, pausing only to send word to his father and uncle telling them what had occurred.

The three Yorkist leaders, from their key strongholds – Salisbury at Middleham in north Yorkshire, Richard Plantagenet at Ludlow in the Welsh Marches, and Warwick from Calais, gathered strength and watched and waited. Meanwhile, Henry Beaufort who now clearly led the Queen's faction, recruited in the southwest and John, Lord Clifford, followed suit in the northwest of the land. Confrontation must come soon and Beaufort and Clifford were determined that, in the final accounting, their fathers' blood would be avenged and family honour vindicated. It was no longer a question of "if the chance comes", merely one of "when".

Queen Margaret herself was far from inactive in seeking renewed strength for Lancaster. Realising that her own drawing-power as a leader of forces dedicated to the fortunes of her adopted House was limited, she used the name and insignia of her only child, Edward of Lancaster, grandson of the great Harry of Monmouth, to attract support. Edward's personal badge involved an ostrich feather with a swan and a crown and this was developed into a "Livery of swans" which was bestowed on knights and gentlemen of Cheshire – traditional recruiting ground for Lancaster – against their pledged loyalty. The Livery was conferred in special ceremonies involving sacred vows of allegiance to the crown, and key Livery-men were subsequently knighted by the King to strengthen further their commitment to the royal cause.

By the late summer of 1459, the Queen believing that her forces were now strong enough to destroy her enemies entirely, ordered her nobles to rally to the King's standard in south Staffordshire. Henry Beaufort, now leading several thousand well-equipped troops from the westcountry commenced his march north in early September. As he was passing through Coleshill, north of Birmingham, three weeks later, he had an urgent summons from Margaret to hasten towards the rendezvous. The Queen's anxiety stemmed from the defeat of a stronger force of Lancastrian troops, led by Lords Audley and Dudley, by Richard Neville, Earl of Salisbury at a place called Blore Heath on the 23rd of the month. Salisbury had moved on to Ludlow and joined there with his brother-in-law, the Duke of York. The two of them now waited on the arrival of Salisbury's son, Richard of Warwick, who was understood to be en route, bringing with him a strong division from his Calais garrison to reinforce the Yorkist army.

The Duke of Somerset immediately speeded the pace of his column towards Stafford, quickly leaving Coleshill behind. Had he not done so, he could well have met with the force Warwick was leading northwest towards the Marches, in the town and probably have defeated it there very easily since, although the Calais contingent were all picked men, they numbered only 600 against the several thousand led by Henry Beaufort. Learning of the proximity of the foe, Warwick swung sharply westwards, away from Somerset's line of march and, by the beginning of October, had joined his kinsmen in the safety of Ludlow's massive Keep. Their sanctuary would shortly prove illusory, however, since Warwick's obvious concern to avoid meeting a division of the King's army, led by the Duke of Somerset, had aroused the curiosity of the chief captain of the Calais men, a veteran of the French Wars called Andrew Trollope. He had been told by Warwick that they were embarking for England to aid the King in putting down a rebel force and, cautious as he was experienced, Trollope had thought it might be well to find how the land really lay. On leaving Coleshill for the west, therefore, he had secretly sent a trusted aide after the Duke of Somerset's host with instructions to have private discourse with Henry Beaufort.

The leaders of the Yorkist faction were reunited in Ludlow during the early days of October. It soon became clear that they could not maintain their force of several thousand within the Castle walls and York ordered a move into the open country south of the town, where they threw up defensive earthworks at Ludford. Here they awaited the appearance of the royal army, which arrived in overwhelming force on October 12th. York immediately sent to the King a lengthy justification of his, and his relatives' actions, protesting their loyalty and complaining of slanders by Somerset and other Lords. On Henry Beaufort's suggestion, King Henry replied that he accepted their loyal protestations and would give them grace of their lives and their goods if they would immediately surrender themselves to his mercy. Certain persons, named as being involved in the deaths of Lord Audley and his men at and after Blore Heath, were excepted from the prospect of pardon, which ensured its non-acceptance by York and Salisbury.

With nightfall approaching, the two armies settled down in facing lines to await events in the morning. Not all was still on the Yorkist side, however, for during the formal exchanges between Richard of York and King Henry, a less-formal contact had been made with Andrew Trollope by a messenger from Henry Beaufort. Beaufort welcomed Trollope's realisation that he and his men had been led from Calais by Warwick to strengthen the rebel forces then gathering and assured him of his personal intercession with the King, if Trollope would lead his men into the royal camp. At dead of night, the captain from Calais led his 600 men away from their position guarding the right flank of the earthworks and crossed no-man's land to where Somerset waited to welcome them.

The rest of York's diminished army, realising quickly what had happened, started to disappear in all directions away from Somerset's waiting host. When dawn broke, the Yorkist works were entirely deserted and the Duke of York, with his second son, Edmund, Earl of Rutland, was heading west for the sure sanctuary of his Irish estates. The Nevilles, Salisbury and Warwick, had turned south making for the Channel coast and thence to Calais, where William Neville, Lord Fauconberg, held the port against his nephew's return. With them rode Edward, Earl of March, York's eldest son and heir.

A triumphant Duke of Somerset led the royal army into Ludlow and there found Cecily, Duchess of York, who was arrested together with her two younger sons, George and Richard. The royal party then moved on to Coventry, where a Parliament was hastily summoned and met on November 20th to attaint the four absent leaders of the Yorkists of treason and to order confiscation of their lands and wealth. Cecily and her boys were placed in the custody of her older sister, Anne, Duchess of Buckingham and, since she was now effectively penniless, King Henry ordered provision of a thousand marks a year to pay for their upkeep.

Following the necessary Acts of Attainder, pauperising the Yorkist nobles, Henry Beaufort was appointed Captain of Calais in Warwick's place and set out in December to take over his new command. Unfortunately for him, and for Lancaster, Warwick with his father, Salisbury, and Edward of March, had made port a few days earlier and when Somerset appeared in Calais roads and demanded that the keys should be handed over to him, he met with a very negative response. Somerset had with him, Andrew Trollope and his men from the Calais garrison and, on their advice, made for Guisnes, from where they could attack Calais overland. Even more unhappily for his cause, however, a storm blew up the Channel which scattered his fleet and, while most of his men landed safely in Guisnes, the vessels carrying their supplies, horses and armour had to take shelter in Calais harbour, where they were eagerly seized by Warwick.

With Somerset effectively out of the game so long as he was blockaded in Guisnes, the court made plans for a relieving fleet, which was to be commanded by the husband of the Queen's greatest friend, Jacquetta, Duchess of Bedford, namely Richard Woodville, Lord Rivers, and his son Sir Anthony. The relief force was expected to sail early in the new year, but the plan was spoiled, through the intervention of two of Warwick's captains, John Dynham and John Wenlock, who sailed into Sandwich harbour very early in the morning of January 15th 1460, took possession of all the ships allocated to the invasion fleet, and captured Rivers in his bed. The intrepid pair then returned to Calais with the prisoners and prizes, where Rivers was thoroughly rated successively by the Earls as a nobody, made by marriage and with no drop of royal blood in his veins. All of which was correct and, with the exception of the blood-royal, might have been argued to be equally true of his Neville captors, but Rivers was diplomat enough not to dispute the point.

The Woodvilles spent five months in captivity, before being taken back to England, in the train of the three Earls, who invaded England on June 27th, accompanied this time by Fauconberg and 2,000 men-at-arms and archers. The Woodvilles were set free while the Earls quickly gathered strength enough in Kent to march on, and occupy, London. Then, while Warwick and Edward of March moved north at the head of a formidable army, to meet the King, leaving Salisbury holding the capital, Henry Beaufort sailed from Guisnes and landed in the westcountry. Here he linked with Courtenay, Earl of Devon and again started recruiting men for the coming armed struggle with the Yorkists, which clearly was now unavoidable. Both sides would probably have agreed that open warfare was preferable as an alternative to the constant swings of Fortune which had preceded it. Neither, however, could possibly have foreseen the true awfulness of what was to come in the nine months following.

CHAPTER NINE

"War, war is still the cry, 'War even to the knife'."
[Childe Harold's Pilgrimage]

Henry Beaufort had barely commenced recruiting in the west, when news came that the King and a strong Lancastrian army had been badly beaten at Northampton on July 10th 1460. Edward of March, leading the Yorkist vanguard, had broken through the King's defences, thanks to the treachery of Lord Grey of Ruthyn, whose men had joined with Edward's as the Calais troops had joined Somerset at Ludford. The King's main division, outflanked and broken, had been trapped between their own defensive earthworks and the flooded River Nene behind them and many had died, including the Earl of Shrewsbury, Lords Beaumont and Egremont and King Henry's most loyal servant, Humphrey Stafford, Duke of Buckingham. The triumphant Yorkists had returned to London, taking the King with them and Queen Margaret and her son Edward had fled Coventry with a small following and were reportedly in Wales seeking sanctuary with Jasper Tudor, Earl of Pembroke and half-brother to the King.

Warwick, who was emerging as the chief decision-maker of the Yorkist party, sent urgently to Richard of York in Dublin, urging the vital necessity for him to return to England and attend the London Parliament called for October 7th. The Duke arrived on the 10th with a train of 300 armed men, "suddenly with great pomp and splendour", and marched through the great hall of the Palace of Westminster, where it was customary for the King to meet with his Lords and Commons. He reached the throne and, with a movement charged with significance, laid his hand on the seat of majesty. He then turned to the waiting Lords and Bishops as though inviting their plaudits, but instead, the Archbishop of Canterbury asked whether York wished to go to the King. The Duke replied "I know of no one in the realm who would not more fitly come to me than I to him", indicating clearly thereby, that the House of York's legitimate claim to England's crown, which had lain dormant for more than sixty years, had been rekindled.

There was little support for York's desire to assume the throne, even the Nevilles showed only passing enthusiasm for such aggrandisement of their close relative. However, the Duke persisted and presented his lengthily argued case to the Commons and Lords, who after prolonged discussions, in Parliament, with the judiciary, and with the King, passed into law an Act of Accord. This confirmed Henry VI as King for his own lifetime, but provided that the crown would pass to York and his heirs after Henry's death. Meantime, the attainders of the Coventry Parliament were reversed and York would have the Principality of Wales, with lands to a value of 10,000 marks a year, which he would share with his sons, March and Rutland. On November 8th 1460 York was proclaimed heir-apparent and Lord Protector.

None of the chief actors in this farce could have had any illusions as to the reaction of Margaret of Anjou to the casual signing away of her son's right of succession by her feeble spouse. The she-wolf of France would do whatever she must to reverse this decree and would be able to rely on the strong – and strengthening – support of Jasper Tudor in Wales; John, Lord Clifford, and Lord John Neville of the Raby branch of that family in the northwest; Harry Percy, Earl of Northumberland in the northeast and the Borders and, above all, of Henry Beaufort, Duke of Somerset, who had indicated he was ready to bring his men north as soon as summoned.

With winter coming on, Margaret sent couriers to all her allies ordering them to rendezvous with her in Yorkshire, where the fat acres owned by Salisbury and York would sustain the enormous horde of men which was rallying to the call of the House of Lancaster. The Duke of Somerset, with the Earl of Devon and close on a thousand men, moved north and east to join the Queen and together, Margaret of Anjou and Henry Beaufont marched to the East Riding of Yorkshire. Here they took command of the great army which had assembled and waited for the counter move of the Duke of York.

Richard Plantagenet did not keep them waiting long. Enraged by accounts of the looting of his Yorkshire estates and alarmed by the apparent strength of the King's cause in his own Yorkshire heartlands, he decided on a strong expedition north as quickly as possible. His eldest son was sent to the Welsh Marches to recruit men, Warwick would stay in London to guard the capital and enlist support from the southern counties, Salisbury, whose own properties in Yorkshire were also suffering would ride with York. Together, the two leaders of the Yorkist faction, accompanied by their younger sons,

Edmund of Rutland and Sir Thomas Neville, and at the head of 2,500 men rode north out of London on December 9th 1460. Their march was delayed by a brush with Somerset's men near Worksop, but the Yorkist force reached Sandal Castle, York's main fortress in south Yorkshire, on the 21st of the month. Feeling themselves secure within Sandal's mighty walls, York and Salisbury resolved to rest their men and to keep the Christmas feast.

Henry Beaufort had not enjoyed the celebration of Christ's birth having fallen sick immediately after the encounter with the Yorkist army. Effective command of the Lancastrian hordes, under the Queen, had therefore devolved on John, Lord Clifford and it was to him, at Pontefract on December 29th, that scouts brought news of the presence of York and Salisbury in Sandal Keep. They had also noted that strong foraging parties were being sent out from the Castle, indicating that supplies inside were short, a factor which could give an important advantage to an army with no siege equipment.

Under Margaret's urging, Clifford rallied as many of his own forces as were close to hand and, the following morning rode off to Sandal, 12 miles to the west. By the mid-afternoon of December 30th 1460, his array had formed in three divisions in the flat plain before Sandal, cutting off the return of the foragers to their base and, worse still, preventing new supplies reaching the main Yorkist force.

York and Salisbury quickly realised their dilemma when they saw the strength of the Lancastrian force formed up below them. In the centre, they saw the royal standard and the "checkies" of Clifford, on the enemy right, another formidable division was led by James Butler, fugitive from First St Albans and Earl of Wiltshire, and on the other side Thomas, Lord Roos, step-brother to Somerset through the marriage between his father and Eleanor Beauchamp, widowed at First St Albans. If York and his brother-in-law waited, their foraging parties would be massacred in sight of the castle walls, their men would go hungry for want of the supplies appropriated by the Queen's army and ultimate defeat was certain. Their only course was to sally out from the castle and, by charging in column, either drive their enemies away or, at worst, force a passage through to safety.

As the shortening day began to turn to twilight, the massive gates of Sandal were flung back and a long procession of armoured riders emerged, quickly forming into column and, led by the banners of York and Salisbury, charged straight for the heart of the enemy line. Their initial impact drove the

WAKEFIELD. DECEMBER 30th 1460.

Calder.

WILTSHIRE

MARGARET & CLIFFORD

YORK

ROOS

Sandal Magna Church.

Wakefield.

N

centre of Clifford's division back and, for a brief moment, it seemed the forlorn hope might break the wall of men and horses facing them and live to fight another day. But the sheer weight of numbers opposed to them was too much and, as the divisions on either flank of their charge closed in to support their centre, the men of York were overrun and quickly killed. More than 3,000 men died in that brief hour as the daylight faded.

Richard Plantaganet, Duke of York, he who would be King, died in or immediately after the fighting. His son, Edmund of Rutland, got through the enemy ranks and reached Wakefield bridge before his pursuers caught and killed him. Thomas Neville, likewise, was slain in the general carnage. Richard Neville, Earl of Salisbury, was wounded in the charge, but survived the battle and was taken on Somerset's orders to Pontefract Castle to be held for ransom. By morning however, news of Salisbury's whereabouts had come to the knowledge of "common people which loved him not" and the old Earl, victor of Blore Heath, eldest son of Joan Beaufort, grandson of John of Gaunt, was dragged out into the courtyard and summarily done to death.

Her major accounts settled, Margaret of Anjou and a recovered Henry Beaufort, prepared to turn their massive army southwards towards the capital for the ultimate confrontation which would see the final restoration of Lancaster's dominion. Before setting out on their march, however, Margaret visited her sister-monarch, Mary of Guelders, queen mother of Scotland at Lincluden Abbey. Here a marriage was arranged between Edward of Lancaster, Prince of Wales, and Mary, sister of James III of Scotland. Queen Margaret offered to cede Berwick to the Scots as recompense for the arrangement and this was ratified in York on January 20th in the presence of the Earls of Devonshire, Northumberland and Westmorland, Lords Fitzhugh, Neville and Roos, this deputation from the English nobility being led by Henry Beaufort, Duke of Somerset. Their treacherous act concluded, Queen and nobles together set out from the cathedral city to join the Lancastrian forces now gathered south of Wakefield. This enormous army, the largest ever assembled in Britain, straddled the Great North Road by 15 miles either side, and waxed impatient to begin their march southwards to the riches of the capital, which this open-handed Queen had promised them in lieu of pay. Behind them they left the heads of the Nevilles and the Plantagenets impaled above the Micklegate Bar with, around the bloody locks of Richard, lately

Duke of York, a mock-crown of paper and straw. A final insult which, after all else that had transpired in the first three weeks of 1461, made doubly certain that henceforward it would be war to the knife, and the knife to the hilt.

Medallion showing profile of Margaret of Anjou, Queen of England.

(Detail from w.w.w.)

CHAPTER TEN

"...I come to tell you things sith then befall'n
After the bloody fray at Wakefield fought..."

[Henry VI Pt 3]

News of the disaster at Sandal came quickly south to Richard Neville, now de facto Earl of Salisbury as well as of Warwick, and he sent messengers haring towards Ludlow to tell Edward of March, heir to his father's Duchy of York the tragic tale. At the same time, he instructed his young cousin to redouble his recruitment efforts and be prepared to march and join forces in London as soon as Warwick sent word. By the end of January, Edward had assembled a modest army, though poorly equipped in the main, the strongest elements being contingents from long-time retainers of York: William Herbert with his south Welshmen and William Hastings, who brought nearly 800 well-armed troops from the English Midlands to join the Yorkist force.

As he was completing his enlistments, Edward, then basing himself in Hereford, heard of a strong Lancastrian force moving north of him towards Worcester, to cut his route to London. He made for Mortimer's Cross and arrayed his force to obstruct the enemy's passage across the River Lugg. Here he was attacked by superior numbers of better-armed troops led by Jasper Tudor, Earl of Pembroke and James Butler, newly returned from a recruiting drive in his Irish estates around Ormonde. After an initial setback, Edward outfought Pembroke and, with Hastings in support, overwhelmed the main Welsh division and their reserves and drove them back into Wales in flight. He then returned to Hereford where he re-equipped his army with materiel taken after the fight and executed Owen Tudor, father of Jasper and Edmund, by Catherine of France, widow of Henry V. The first blood-repayment for Wakefield being tallied, Edward formed his men into column and started east to join Warwick.

Richard Neville had decided to make his fight at St Albans, perhaps because it had proved a lucky battle-site for him six years earlier. Whatever

Richard Neville, Earl of Warwick, "Kingmaker".

(Original portrait by Ralph Taylor)

his reason, his decision was less than fortunate for the thousands of ordinary people living in the path of the Lancastrian hordes, as they progressed slowly southwards. Refugees fleeing before the advance bore tales of unceasing arson, pillage and rapine with them. It was as though Margaret of Anjou had decided to exact vengeance for the similar treatment, over nearly a century, of French homes and people by English armies. Towns, villages, abbeys and manor houses were pillaged and burned, churches were robbed of vestments and valuables, and farmers and townsmen were tortured to make them reveal where they had hidden their money and crops. Grantham, Peterborough and Stamford paid in full for Warwick's wait-and-see policy, as did Huntingdon, Royston and Melbourne next. At yet one more moment in history, for ordinary Englishmen and women, "God and his saints slept". In one instance only did divine intervention seemingly provide security. The Crowland Chronicler was able to record "Blessed be God who did not give us for a prey unto their teeth".

By mid-February, the army of Lancaster had reached Luton and here they rested, while Somerset and the Queen held a council of war with their commanders. The Lords who had supported the cession of Berwick were still marching alongside their Queen and her generalissimo, Henry Beaufort, joined now by rough, surly John Clifford who had stayed with the army after Wakefield, eager to begin the southward march, as had Andrew Trollope, the captain from Calais, who would be unlikely to survive capture by Warwick or Edward. The army of Lancaster had taken close on a month to reach a point 30 miles north of the capital and Somerset had ordered scouts to be sent south and west to locate the Earl of Warwick and his army. When their reports came in the final plan of attack would be laid down.

On St Valentine's Day, a Kentish squire, Lovelace, sent intelligence to the Queen that Warwick had marched from London, headed for St Albans, taking King Henry with him, to give some semblance of legality to the Yorkists' objective of "punishing the northern Rebels". In the afternoon of February 16th 1461, scouts galloped hard-ridden horses to the Queen's headquarters in Luton with news of a force of enemy cavalry, strong enough to be Warwick's advance guard, only five miles away at Dunstable. On Margaret's orders, Beaufort marshalled the army and moved quickly westwards to engage the enemy, only to find that the "strong force" was made up of 200 horsemen scouting for the Yorkist main body.

Forceful interrogation of their prisoners yielded the news that Warwick was standing on the defensive at St Albans, barring the road to London and, although evening was drawing on, the Queen was adamant that her chief enemy be brought to battle at the earliest possible moment. Henry Beaufort, his army of some 40,000 already drawn up in marching order, saw sense in continuing the move to engage Warwick and decided a night march to St Albans with a view to a surprise attack at dawn, was worth the risk. And so, as the evening shadows darkened, the Duke of Somerset set out southwards towards the town where his father had died six years before. Leading his advance guard were John Clifford and Harry Percy, both likewise made fatherless at First St Albans, and with them marched Lord John Neville of the family's Westmorland branch, leading the 8,000 Scottish Border reivers he had raised under licence from the dead Duke of York.

Richard Neville, Earl of Warwick was, by nature, a consummate politician and, since the deaths of his father and uncle at Wakefield, the richest peer in England. Now in his thirty-third year, he was the accepted leader of the Yorkist party and chief mentor of his young cousin Edward. He had built an impressive military reputation at and since First St Albans and had studied the art of war assiduously, including the use of new weaponry: ground-nets with long nails knotted vertically in them, shields fitted with shutters through which archers might shoot, and others with long nails protruding from them, which could be thrown down before a charging enemy to form a primitive "minefield". In brief, he was a master of policy, planning and logistics, but had one unfortunate shortcoming as a military leader. Like so many of his Beaufort kin, his ability as a fighting general in the field was not merely limited, it was non-existent.

Arrived at St Albans on February 12th and aware from refugees and his scouts' reports that Margaret was coming steadily south, he had decided he must block the two main approaches from the north, namely the roads from Harpenden and Luton. With little more than 20,000 men at his disposal he could not make a line four miles across and, instead, divided his force into four divisions. The first consisted of a strong group of Yorkshire archers which he based in the centre of the town, while the second and strongest division he positioned in an old earthwork, a mile up the Luton road. A mile further north, on the Harpenden road at a village called Sandridge, he placed a third detachment. His fourth and last section anchored the right of his line another mile still to the north at, in light of coming events, a place unhappily named by the local inhabitants as "No Man's Land".

On the night of February 16th, Warwick checked his troop dispositions and, deciding they were satisfactory, retired to bed, where he slept soundly. Perhaps he would have done neither had a more experienced general been present to point out his two cardinal errors: he had divided his force in the face of an advancing enemy and his whole army was facing in the wrong direction. So, the Earl of Warwick's wakening was rude indeed, a sudden clash of arms and then a swelling roar of battle from the centre of the town, which told that the Yorkshiremen had kept better watch than their general and were driving their assailants back the way they had come.

Clifford and Neville had reached the undefended west approach to St Albans by first light and, without pausing for rest, had led their columns straight down Fishpool Street, past the Abbey and into the town square. Warwick's archers, alerted by the din of Lancaster's approach, quickly roused, formed line and threw the enemy's first onslaught back in confusion. Their triumph was brief, however, for still more attackers had made their way down Catherine Street and now emerged behind the Yorkist line. As the archers turned to meet this new threat, the first assault was renewed and, beset from both sides, they had no choice but to sell their lives dearly in the hope that relief would come.

The anticipation of help would prove vain, for the Earl of Warwick, having armed himself as best and as quickly as he could, was pre-occupied with the re-arrangement of his main defensive line. This had to be moved from the old earthwork on the Luton road, to face down the Harpenden road into the town, taking with it as much of Warwick's advanced weaponry as could be moved at the double. The archers, in their dying, gave the second line time to complete preparations to face another attack, and the Lancastrians gave them more by settling down to their customary pillaging of the town, intermingled with eating and drinking. Shortly before noon, Somerset had enough of them in hand to order an advance past St Peter's Church and up the slope to where the new line awaited their onset.

Urged on by the Queen and Henry Beaufort, the army of Lancaster

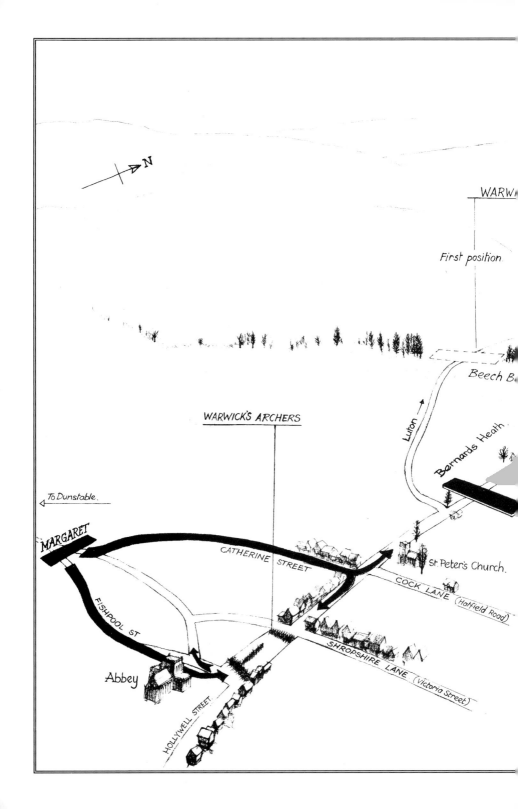

N

WARW[...]

First position.

Beech B[...]

WARWICK'S ARCHERS

Luton

Barnards Heath.

To Dunstable.

MARGARET

CATHERINE STREET

St Peter's Church.

COCK LANE (Hatfield Road)

FISHPOOL ST

Abbey

HOLLYWELL STREET

SHROPSHIRE LANE (Victoria Street)

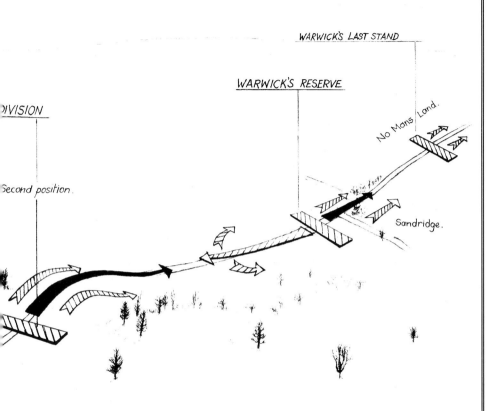

WARWICK'S LAST STAND

WARWICK'S RESERVE

DIVISION

Second position.

No Mans Land.

Sandridge.

Second St. ALBANS.
February 17th 1461.

charged in a long, wide column and threw themselves at the waiting Yorkists. Initially the fight went well for Warwick's men, and the enemy was thrown back time and again, with the new paraphernalia proving a serious hindrance to the assaulting troops. Growing in confidence, the Yorkist men were content to hold their ground and await the arrival of their comrades in the third division, whom Warwick was at that very moment in the act of persuading to move up the slope from Sandridge and join the battle. Unhappily for him, and for the men already fully engaged, the Sandridge contingent was hesitant about leaving their established position, many thinking it better to hold their ground and await any attack which might get through the second line.

Using all his considerable powers of persuasion, Warwick finally convinced the reluctant troops that their best course lay in reinforcing the ongoing fight their comrades were making over the hilltop. They formed lines and started to advance up the gentle slope towards the continuing roar of battle, as the Earl of Warwick turned wearily away from the fighting yet again, to bring up his last reserves from No Man's Land. Too late. The wavering of the men at Sandridge had lasted too long. The strong, second line under incessant attack, sadly outnumbered and weary of waiting for help which did not come, had lost heart and now, as the third division began its advance to join the fight, a fleeing, broken horde of Yorkists, intermingled with brawling, killing, Lancastrian pursuers, burst over the ridge and cascaded down the hill, shattering the relieving lines into broken remnants in their course.The second battle at St Albans was over and triumphing Lancastrians hailed their general, Henry Beaufort, Duke of Somerset, as victor over the perfidious Earl of Warwick.

Richard Neville, realising that all was lost, had already turned his face and the remnants of his army westwards, in the hope of linking with his cousin Edward's command. King Henry VI was found by units of his rescuers under the shelter of a tree in No Man's Land. Abandoned by the fleeing Warwick, he was guarded only by Sir Thomas Kyriel, a veteran commander of the French wars in Henry's service, and his son, both of whom, he told his Queen, "had used him kindly". This did not avail to temper the mood of his consort, angered that her victory should be marred by Warwick's escaping her just vengeance. She asked her young son, Edward, "Fair son, by what manner of death shall these knights die?" To which the seven-year-old Prince of Wales replied that their heads should be chopped off. Over the futile, feeble protests of the newly-liberated monarch, the boy's sentence was carried out without more ado.

The huge, ill-disciplined army settled for the night in the town, where they had avenged Lancaster's first defeat five years earlier, and occupied themselves for some days in looting the surrounding area and replenishing their supplies. By the time the men had been assembled again and the army approached London, the Queen found the gates barred against her and the city held by a strong force commanded by Warwick and Edward of York, who had come together at Burford and raced for the capital with all possible speed. Their opportunity missed and without essential siege equipment, the disappointed Lancastrians had no other course but to turn north again, where they could rest and resupply and await the next, inevitable clash. In the following battle however, the enemy would have a new leader in the young Earl of March, latterly Duke of York and now, new-crowned King of England. Edward, fourth of that name to rule the land and not yet twenty years old, would teach the Lords of Lancaster how war was made.

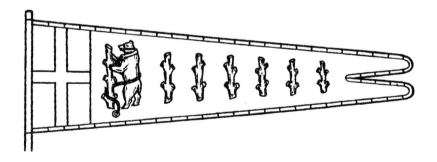

CHAPTER ELEVEN

"...This Battle fares like to the morning's war
When dying clouds contend with growing light..."
[Henry VI Pt 3]

The great host of Lancaster did not make a leisurely retreat to their northern base in York. Their ravaging of the land on the way south meant that remaining stocks of grains and fodder, cattle and sheep were few and better hidden than a month earlier. Thus, Henry Beaufort, victor of St Albans, was back in York with the bulk of his army before the end of the first week in March and the last stragglers were coming in. Overall, Beaufort could count on 40,000 men with which to fight the next battle and he was content to wait on the coming of the new King of England. Edward did not keep him long and on the 25th of March, scouts came in with news that a mighty Yorkist army was gathering at Pontefract, less than twenty miles south of the walls of York. Lancaster's victorious troops were ordered to assemble and, early on Friday March 27th, with Lord John Clifford commanding the vanguard, the Duke of Somerset marched his army south-westwards along the road Edward must come.

Halfway to Pontefract, he came to a ridge commanding a wide tableland just beyond a tiny village called Towton. Here Somerset decided he would make his fight and, with his commanders, Exeter and Wiltshire, Northumberland and Dacre, John Neville and Beaumont and Trollope, he set about deploying the mighty mass of men across the chosen ground. This would be a lengthy task and Clifford was sent forward with a strong force of mounted archers to guard the crossing of the River Aire at Ferrybridge and, at need, to delay the Yorkist advance there.

Clifford reached the crossing by nightfall and deployed his men in an ambush on the north side of the river, where they settled to await developments. At first-light they heard the clatter of approaching horsemen and, in the midst of the strong cavalry advance guard, saw a banner bearing the white saltire on a red ground of the Nevilles, quartered with the red lozenges of Montacute. It was the Earl of Warwick himself leading the van of the Yorkist army against Henry Beaufort and John Clifford. The latter wasted little time in ordering his men to open fire and their arrow-shelfs brought men and horses crashing to the ground on the opposite bank of the Aire. Warwick himself suffered only a minor wound in the knee and led the charge away from the crossing and back to report to King Edward, now well forward from Pontefract.

Swinging down from his mount, favouring his wounded member, Richard Neville reported that the crossing at Ferrybridge was held in great strength and that crossing the river there would be perilous in the extreme. However, for his part, he would take not one more step back, in token of which he drew his sword and killed his sweat-lathered horse with a blow. Edward, unimpressed by these histrionics, ordered Fauconberg to find an alternative crossing point upriver from the ambush and led the bulk of the army forward towards Ferrybridge. Warwick brought up the rearguard, leaving behind John Mowbray, Duke of Norfolk, who was sick, but swore he would follow the main host with his 5,000 East Anglians as soon as he could sit a horse.

Clifford, hearing the growing rumble of Edward's approach, checked that his men were ready in their positions and awaited his opportunity to kill more of the men of York. Unhappily for him, he did not suspect that his ambush had been rendered vulnerable by that experienced soldier, William Neville, Lord Fauconberg,who had easily found a crossing point at Castleford, two miles upstream of Ferrybridge, and was now moving quietly and purposefully towards Clifford's right flank and rear. As soon as Edward with the main force approached the crossing, Neville ordered his archers to loose and, under the hail of arrows, the surprised Clifford at last realised his peril and ordered a hurried retreat back up the road to Towton. The bulk of the men reached their horses, leaped into the saddles, and galloped furiously away towards their main force, but their commander was not so fortunate. As he turned to follow his archers, he was caught in the neck by a Yorkist shaft and badly hurt. His lieutenants supported him in the saddle and tried to bring him to the safety of the lines before Towton, but his wound was mortal and he died somewhere along the narrow track through Dintingdale and Saxton as his surviving archers made good their escape. His warlike fervour would be sadly missed by the army of Lancaster during the bloody day to come.

Henry Beaufort was dismayed to hear that Lancaster's cause had lost its fiercest partisan and, as the cold grey evening advanced, he saw the mighty host of York climb the track from the Ferrybridge road up to the ridge on the farther side of Towton Dale and make its way across to the woods on Castle Hill above the ravine cut by the Cock Beck. A great army indeed and the hour was late and his men chilled to the bone. He would make no move now; better to wait on the morning light, then stand fast and dare the usurper to attack his position. Yes, that would be the best course. And so, the two greatest armies England would ever see assembled settled for the night, sheltering as best they could from the cutting wind and the snow flurries blowing in it.

With the bleak dawn the long lines of men rose and stamped the circulation back into their feet and legs, chafed their hands, clapped their arms, anything to bring some warmth into their frozen limbs. Then they dressed their ranks and looked towards the foe opposite, waiting for the first move. The archers were advanced on both sides to take their customary toll of the first charge by the enemy and shouts of defiance were exchanged, but neither army made any move towards the other. Both would await the other's attack on their strong position as their forefathers had done facing a common enemy at Crecy and Poitiers and Agincourt.

Towards 11 o'clock, Somerset peering through the wind-driven snow blasts saw movement along the Yorkist front, Fauconberg's archers were advancing. Immediately after, a wide shelf of arrows arrived killing and wounding men in the front ranks and his forward commanders, Dacre, Neville and Percy ordered the archers in their front to respond in kind. The Lancastrian bowmen fired volley after volley towards the Yorkist line, unable to see what effect their fire was having due to the snow blowing in their faces and unaware that their opponents had withdrawn 60 paces immediately after firing into the Lancastrian lines. The archery practice of Somerset's men was no more than that and, as Lancaster's ineffective fire slackened for want of ammunition, Fauconberg urged his men forward again to renew their fire on the enemy's lines, reinforcing their own shafts with the spent arrows the enemy had fired unavailingly into the blizzard.

Quickly, this stinging assault from long-range became intolerable to the forward ranks of Lancaster and, heedless of their orders to stand fast and await the Yorkist onset, Somerset's great army lurched forward off its ridge, down into the vale between, and up the slope on the other side towards the

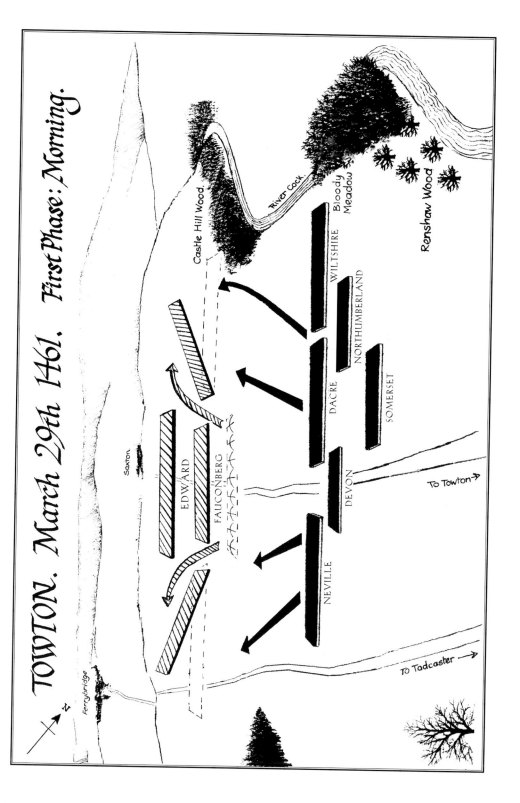

TOWTON. March 29th 1461. First Phase: Morning.

crest lined with killing steel. At about noon, the two lines came together with an enormous clash and the hammering of steel on steel drowned the wailing of the wind and steam rose from the conflicting ranks as the wounding and maiming and killing generated bodily heat into the freezing air. So many were the troops involved that they were able to fight in stints, with weary or wounded men able to make room for the men behind to take their part in the struggle. The killed and the dying, falling between the fighting ranks until heaps of them impeded their still-living comrades, were flung aside or trampled down, to make room for manoeuvre of the troops still engaged in the on-going, never-ending conflict.

And, gradually, bit by bit, death by death, the Lancastrian attack took effect. Their army was more numerous than Edward's, their troops buoyed by the victories at Wakefield and St Albans, and now, urged on by their leaders, they pressed the Yorkist wings back and back with increasingly triumphant shouts. Evening was coming on, York's cause was lost and there could be no recovery from defeat for there was nowhere on that great, flat, blood-grimed plateau where a beaten army might find refuge. And then, suddenly, Somerset heard shouting over to the left, from the Ferrybridge road, trumpets blaring, clashing of arms, and a great, charging column forcing his men off their hard-won place on York's ridge, pushing them back down the slope and across the field into his centre divisions.

From his position in the centre of Lancaster's first position, Henry Beaufort saw his army peel backwards and away from this surprise assault, until their line had turned almost through 90 degrees. Still they were fighting, striving to keep their dressing, struggling to hold together, against the relentless drive of the new-arriving men from East Anglia led by the tardy John Mowbray, Duke of Norfolk. For a moment Beaufort thought they had succeeded in stabilising their line, but, looking down on the conflict from the centre of the opposite ridge was the most decisive commander England had seen, Edward IV, huge in his battered battle-armour and knowing that the critical moment of the bloody struggle had come at last. He urged his centre divisions to one last great effort and they drove Lancaster's quaking centre before them, down the slope into the bottom of Towton Dale and the whole army broke and fled.

As always with broken, exhausted men, they took the easy route, downhill. Down steep slopes, covered now in snow, soon slimed by blood,

TOWTON. March 29th 1461. Second Phase: Afternoon.

N

Ferrybridge

Saxton

Castle Hill Wood.

River Cock.

Bloody Meadow

Renshaw Wood

NORFOLK

EDWARD

SOMERSET

To Towton →

To Tadcaster →

into the ravine where flowed a flooded Cock Beck. The rains and snows, unending for two weeks, had made the tiny stream flood and race, and tired, armoured men could not safely pass through this torrent. The leaders fell and drowned and when enough of their fellows had joined them in death, their bodies, together, formed human bridges across which their fleeing comrades sought succour away from the murderous swords and knives and arrows of the pursuing Yorkists.

Henry Beaufort, luckier than his men, had his horse to hand and escaped more quickly from the stricken field, through Tadcaster and back to York. Back with the sad news, to King Henry and his Queen, of the destruction of their great army and the ruin of all their hopes. Then on with them further, to Scotland and its fleeting, uncertain security, to await better times and plan another challenge from Lancaster for the crown of England. Somerset left behind him, united now only in death, Harry Percy, third Earl of Northumberland, Lord John Neville, Lords Dacre, Wells and Willoughby and, making payment in full for his treachery two years earlier, Captain Andrew Trollope. Courtenay of Devon was caught and beheaded after the fight and James Butler, successful fugitive from First St Albans, and Blore Heath, also escaped Towton's awful aftermath, but was recognised in Cockermouth days later, making his way north to the Border country, and was beheaded on the personal order of the new Monarch.

Beaufort's conqueror, Edward, now undoubted King of England, wrote home to his mother of his triumph and the 28,000 lives it had cost. He ordered arrangements for the dead to be interred in mass graves, not knowing – how could he – that among them was the stripped and unidentified corpse of Sir John Grey, Lord Ferrers of Groby, lately, husband of Elizabeth Woodville, and then turned his horse's head towards London and the triumphal celebrations which awaited him there.

Thus was the Anniversary of Christ's triumphal entry into Jerusalem celebrated in Yorkshire, on Palm Sunday in the year of our Lord, 1461.

CHAPTER TWELVE

"...so manly a man is this good Earl Montagu, for he spared not their...treason and took many men and slew many a one that day..."

[Gregory's Chronicle.]

Two months after her flight to Scotland, Margaret of Anjou brought 6,000 Scots over the western Border to sack Carlisle, which she had promised to cede to Scotland in return for military support, as she had done with Berwick the year before. Their attack was anticipated, however, and John Neville, Lord Montagu, waiting until the Scottish siege-works were under way, made a sudden surprise attack and drove the invaders, helter-skelter, back over the Border, with heavy loss of men and materiel. Subsequently, following the strategy laid down by his brother Richard, Earl of Warwick, in his new capacity as Warden of the Western and Eastern Marches, the two Nevilles worked their way eastwards across the northern counties, eliminating pockets of Lancastrian resistance along the way and, by the end of October, they had taken Alnwick and Dunstanburgh, the two great strongholds of the Percies. With most of Northumberland at peace, Warwick left Montagu to keep watch and ward and answered Edward's summons to a November Parliament at Westminster.

Early in the following year, a conspiracy was discovered to assassinate the King. The plan was to draw Edward north to deal with renewed invasion from Scotland and to kill him on the march. Unfortunately for the plotters, their scheme had been discovered in its early stages and before it could be fully implemented, the leader of the plot, John de Vere, 12th Earl of Oxford, with his eldest son, was arrested in early February and the pair were summarily executed. Nevertheless, despite this early setback, the supporters of Lancaster continued with the balance of their plot to restore Henry VI to his throne. Henry Beaufort, who had been in Burgundy and France canvassing support, arrived in Scotland at about the time of Oxford's execution and proceeded to draw exiled Lancastrians and plunder-hungry Scots into an invasion force.

Richard Neville, alerted by his agents at the Scottish court, moved north to his Yorkshire base and sent to Mary of Guelders, queen mother in Scotland, proposing marriage alliances between her son and daughter and Edward's siblings and scouted the possibility of a further marital bonding between Mary herself and the new King of England. Queen Mary, probably influenced by Somerset, who had joined her coterie of lovers, loaned Margaret of Anjou £300 to finance a voyage to France, where she hoped to persuade the new King, Louis XI, to provide her with men and money to aid Lancaster's cause. Meantime, Mary of Guelders kept Warwick in play for as long as possible, but her game-plan soon became obvious, to one equally devious. Having used the interval to make his own preparations, Warwick ordered Montagu to move into Scotland, where the two Nevilles implemented a scorched earth policy to such effect that the Scots sued for peace and a summer truce was signed at Carlisle in the month of June.

In October, Margaret of Anjou arrived back in the north country, accompanied by Piers de Brézé, Seneschal of Normandy, with a token force of French troops supplied by Louis, who clearly did not expect to gain much from the venture, although he had a treaty signed by Margaret returning ownership of Calais to the French crown, in the event that her invasion succeeded. The force, having linked with Beaufort at Bamburgh, advanced into Northumberland hoping to recruit from the local population. In this they were disappointed, though they succeeded in taking Alnwick and Dunstanburgh and when they heard of Edward approaching with a strong army, Margaret lost no time in sending her husband back into Scotland overland, and taking to the sea again herself, with their treasure, bound for the north. Again, this most misfortunate of Queens was overtaken by disaster when a storm blew up and her carrack was wrecked, her treasure lost, and she herself narrowly escaping with her life in a fishing boat.

Henry Beaufort had been left in command of the territorial gains, such as they were, and shut himself and his small army in Dunstanburgh and Bamburgh. Here they were besieged by Warwick, who, whatever his failings as a field commander, was a master of siege-warfare and, on the two days following Christmas, both castles surrendered. The men and officers gave up their weapons and were allowed to depart; Lord Roos, Sir Ralph Percy and Jasper Tudor, Earl of Pembroke, were to have their estates restored, having

Edward IV

(Original portrait by Ralph Taylor)

sworn allegiance to Edward; but Henry, Duke of Somerset, head of the House of Beaufort, was sent to his King for judgement at Durham, where Edward was recovering from an attack of measles. Here, Beaufort exercised all his Plantagenet charm on the recuperating Monarch and Edward, wishing for nothing more than a peaceful realm to govern, forgave all past misdeeds and took the Duke of Somerset as his boon companion, at board and in bed from thenceforth.

Meanwhile, Warwick had turned his attentions to the siege of Alnwick and had taken personal command of his troops there. On January 8th 1463, alarmed by reports of a relieving Scottish force led by the Earl of Angus, he immediately summoned his men to horse and rode off, not towards the approaching foe, but in exactly the opposite direction. The hard-pressed defenders of the castle were ecstatic at their deliverance and sallied out of their fortress to greet Angus and persuade him to join with them in pursuit of the fleeing Yorkists. Unhappily for their hopes, Angus, a shrewd Border Scot, sensed some kind of trap lurking and decided he would withdraw his men back over the Border. The garrison had little option but to join him in retreat and, a few days later, Warwick, returning warily to the scene, found the castle open to his approach and scored a bloodless – and totally undeserved – victory.

At Shrovetide 1463, King Edward was recovered sufficiently to return to London and he took Henry Beaufort with him. Edward ensured that Somerset's titles and estates were restored to him by the spring Parliament and, thereafter, the two men were constantly in each other's company; they ate together, hunted together and, often times, Beaufort shared the royal bed, a mark of particular favour. During these months of good fellowship, Edward ordered a Grand Tourney at Westminster in honour of his cousin and encouraged a reluctant Somerset to take part in the jousting, hoping thereby to cheer him, for he sensed a remoteness within his former enemy, which he felt it essential to dispel, and, for a time, it seemed his efforts were successful.

At the end of June, news arrived from Montagu, watching the north for his King, of a new incursion by a strong, mixed band of Scots, French and Lancastrians led by de Brézé, which had summoned the three main castles and received immediate surrender from their garrisons. The invaders had then moved on to take Norham Castle, and the Earl of Warwick, who had been attending the spring Parliament, returned north immediately to support his brother. The Nevilles relieved Norham and drove the besieging army off in complete disarray, such that the Scots did not halt until they were over the Border, while de Brézé and his French took to their ships and fled to Flanders, taking Margaret of Anjou and the remaining shell of her court with them. Henry VI was left behind and made his way, with difficulty, to Bamburgh.

During July, Edward determined to visit the north of his kingdom to see for himself how his people had been affected by the renewed unrest and accompanying him was Henry Beaufort as commander of his personal guard. Although the King had gone out of his way, time and again in the preceding months, to show his trust in Somerset and to demonstrate his forgiveness for past differences, efforts which had been fully reciprocated by the Duke, the great mass of English people were unwilling to believe in such a bizarre conversion. Many remembered that Henry Beaufort had led the massive Lancastrian army on its wide-passage of looting, murder and rapine from York to London only two years earlier and there were blood-debts a-plenty still to be paid.

The royal train arrived in Northampton during the last week in July and, as the party settled for the evening, a growing mob assembled around the King's lodgings, demanding that the Duke of Somerset should be handed over to them for justice. Edward, ever a King with the common touch, went out to reason with his people and he jested with them and cast largesse among them and ordered tuns of wine to be broached in the surrounding streets, all of which combined to change a threatening mood into a festive occasion and a lynch-mob into a massive street-party. But, his object achieved, Edward did not try the patience of his subjects again. Instead the guard, which was dressed in Somerset's colours, was sent immediately to Newcastle and the Duke himself slipped out of the town and made his way, secretly, towards Wales, where both he and his King deemed he would be more secure. The two cousins would never meet again.

By December, Henry Beaufort had recognised the impossibility of forsaking his inbred loyalty to Lancaster and set out northeast towards Newcastle, where he planned to create further conflict for his erstwhile friend and Sovereign. In Durham, he was recognised and men loyal to Edward went to take him while he slept. He was warned just in time and escaped in his shirt, losing money and harness but saving his life. His followers in Newcastle, hearing of this near-disaster, slipped out of the city to join him, but some of them were caught and paid the capital penalty for their loyalty to a cause already lost.

At Easter, the Scots, suffering from Montagu's counter-blows, were ready to sue for peace again and, King Edward agreeing, they were invited to send commissioners to meet Edward's nominees at York to discuss a treaty. Beaufort, having recovered clothing and communications by this time, got wind of these arrangements and ordered Sir Humphrey, brother of Lord John Neville killed at Towton, and Sir Ralph Percy to join with him in ambushing Montagu as he travelled to Newcastle to meet the Scottish emissaries. The new Warden of the Eastern Marches had his own sources of information however and learned of the plot in time to take a different route to Newcastle. There he found reinforcements and went looking for his would-be attackers, whom he caught on April 25th at Hedgeley Moor and scattered to the four winds. Humphrey Neville escaped to fight again, Ralph Percy, less fortunate, died in the skirmishing, while Henry Beaufort, elusive as always on a broken field, made his way to safe haven by the Roman Wall, where he was joined by Henry VI.

Meantime, Montagu had collected the Scottish commissioners and conducted them without further mishap to York, where his two brothers, Richard of Warwick and George, Chancellor of England, commenced negotiations on a 15 year truce with the Scots. Whilst these talks were taking place, John Neville moved back to his chief base at Newcastle, whence his spies had brought word of renewed stirring along the Border in the cause of Lancaster. On arrival he learned that Somerset, with King Henry and part of the Bamburgh garrison, had raised a small army which had made its base on Hexham Levels, a patch of flat land located in a bend of a steeply-banked, fast-flowing stream called the Devil's Water. Neville ordered out his whole force of three to four thousand cavalry and moved west along the 15 miles of road which separated him from the incessant irritation provided by Henry Beaufort, Duke of Somerset.

Somerset had made his camp in an apparently easily defensible site with one side and both flanks protected by the curving ravine through which the Devil's Water raced. Unhappily, the one open side faced directly east

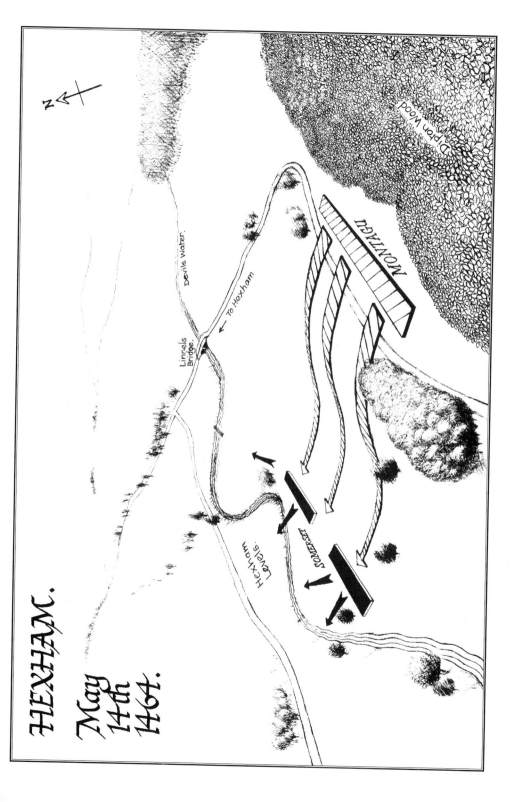

which was the most likely direction for any hostile force to approach, coming from a Newcastle base. This error of judgement was brought to Henry Beaufort's attention on May 14th 1464, less than three weeks after his escape from the abortive ambush at Hedgeley Moor, when he was apprised by gallopers coming in from the Newcastle road, that a large force of cavalry was approaching his base. He arrayed his army of little more than 2,000 men in two divisions in front of his camp, covering the open flank of the site and, too late, realised there was a further disadvantage to his chosen location. Immediately to his front the ground rose sharply and he was facing a high ridge over which any attack from the east must come.

Soon, the approaching drumming of hooves and rattling of harness materialised into a dense wall of horsemen lining the ridge before and above the Lancastrians and, in the centre of the opposing line, the white saltire on a red ground fluttered above the commanding general. John Neville, Lord Montagu, had come in person to present the last account for Somerset's unbounded loyalty to the cause of Lancaster, and Montagu was not a man to stand on ceremony in such matters. Horns and trumpets sounded and the whole mass of Yorkist horse charged furiously down the hill and into the thin enemy lines before them. The result was never in doubt. Most of Beaufort's force tried to flee without even striking a blow; King Henry scuttled for his life along a sheep-track which passed diagonally across the attackers' front, and only the small group around Somerset tried to cut their way out of the disaster. In vain – their leader was unhorsed and struck down and they died trying to prevent his inevitable capture. In this they were little worse off than their fellows who were caught and killed in flight, or drowned as they tried to leap the chasm of Devil's Water. Few made good their escape and, of the 2,000 dead, nearly all were men of Lancaster.

The leaders were taken by Montagu and his victorious force to Hexham town, where Henry Beaufort, sorely wounded as he was, received quick and merciless justice from Montagu's headsman, as did Sir Edmund Fitzhugh, another enduring Lancastrian, whose grandfather had been Chamberlain to Henry V. Two days later, at Newcastle, Lord Roos, Somerset's step-brother, who had led divisions at Wakefield, Second St Albans and Towton, died with Lord Hungerford, another attainted after Towton, and with three other knights and, days later still, at the Neville stronghold of Middleham, Sir Philip Wentworth, High Sheriff of Norfolk and Suffolk, with six squires, followed their former leader into the darkness. John Neville had made certain that it would be long – if ever – before the banner of Lancaster was raised again to signal revolt in the Border lands.

Royal approval of Montagu's achievement was not overly long in coming. Edward arrived at York on May 27th and, as a mark of his strong approval of recent events, was happy to confer on John Neville the vacant Earldom of Northumberland with most of the land pertaining thereto. He was then graciously pleased to sign the Truce with the Scots, who returned, their mission accomplished, to Edinburgh. To complete the tour of his northern lands, Edward made a stately progress across north Yorkshire to the Nevilles' chief stronghold at Middleham, where he spent time with his two cousins and their families in mutual harmony. It was a pleasant, even idyllic, ending to his journey, but he must have known it could be the last time he would meet with Warwick on such friendly terms for, on his way north, King Edward had secretly taken a wife.

Garter Stall Plate of John Neville, Marquis Montagu.

(St George's Chapel, Windsor)

Part Four

The Betrayed Ones

Charles, Count of Charolais.

(Detail from the w.w.w.)

CHAPTER THIRTEEN

"...When the World turned upside-down..."
[18thC English dance-tune]

With the death of Henry Beaufort, second Duke of Somerset, only three male descendants of the union between John of Gaunt and Katherine Swynford survived. The two senior, in age at least, were Edmund, heir apparent to the family title, who was three years younger than his late brother and John who was barely out of his teens. The third potential inheritor was the sole heir, after his mother, of the senior line of the family, a boy of seven called Henry Tudor, of whom more will be heard. The two younger Beauforts were not with Somerset at Hexham, and fled to France in the late summer of 1464. By the autumn of that year, they had found a poverty-stricken sanctuary as part of Lancaster's "royal" court-in-exile at the castle of Koeur-la-Petite in Lorraine, which belonged to René of Anjou, Queen Margaret's father.

Edmund Beaufort soon wearied of the short commons which were all that Queen Margaret could provide for her followers from the 6,000 French crowns a year pension her father allowed her. Plain fare and thin wine were not to his taste and, by the turn of the year, he had moved to Bruges in search of supply more fitting to his rank as the self-styled Duke of Somerset. Soon he had an opportunity to join an army which Charles, Count of Charolais and heir to the dukedom, was recruiting as part of a greater force being formed by all the Princelings of France under the grandiose designation "The League of the Public Weal". The purpose of the League was to resist new checks on the hitherto almost-boundless powers of the French nobility, which the new King, Louis XI, sought to impose.

The League's army was led by Jean, Duke of Bourbon together with Francis of Brittany, and Charles of Charolais, representing Burgundy, was eager to further his duchy's interests through playing an increasingly important role in the command of the soldiery. By the middle of summer, Charles had established himself as the leading general of the army, which he had encamped near Paris. The royal force, led by Piers de Brézé, was under instruction to slip past the Army of the Public Weal and to enter and fortify the capital against any attempt by the rebel Princes to take it by a coup de main. Unfortunately for Louis' strategy, de Brézé, though aging now, still retained some of his former instincts for battle and a brush with the League's prickers on July 16th 1465 soon developed into a skirmish and thence into a full-scale battle.

The fighting was disjointed, the outcome inconclusive and only two consequences of any note came out of it. The long and adventurous life of Piers de Brézé, Grand Seneschal of Normandy, faithful friend and champion of Margaret of Anjou, the Butcher of Sandwich, was ended by rebel Frenchmen in the fields of Montl'herey. Edmund Beaufort, fighting for the Burgundian side in his first battle, would have noted the abrupt departure of this old Lancastrian ally with some regret, though he would hardly have mentioned this to his new leader Charles, Count of Charolais. The other significant result arising related to Count Charles, who had also fought his first battle and, after ending the day holding the field, concluded that his true vocation in life was the making of war and he carried this belief, unshaken, through successive defeats for the next twelve years, until the Swiss terminated his misplaced ambition, along with his life, at Nancy on January 5th, 1477.

Meanwhile, Charles had succeeded to his father's title as Duke of Burgundy in the middle of June 1467. A year later, almost to the day, Edmund Beaufort, who had learned much of soldiering with the Burgundian armies during the constant engagements, large and small, since the day of Montl'herey, left Charles's court, following the arrival of Margaret of York, sister to Edward IV, and Duchess of Burgundy to be. However, Duke Charles would always keep a soft spot in his heart for the self-styled Duke of Somerset and he continued, secretly, to pay him a pension, while overtly supporting the Yorkist cause.

Despite his exclusion from the general festivities, Somerset was able to make good use of his benefactor's wedding celebrations, through clandestine contact with Lancastrian sympathisers among the many English hangers-on attending. By this means, messages were exchanged with persons highly placed in England, who still looked for the restoration of Henry VI to the throne of his fathers, when fate smiled once more on Lancaster's cause. It was well known amongst the English exiles living in and around the Burgundian court that the powerful Earl of Warwick had worked long and hard for a marriage alliance with France and, although he had carried the new Duchess, pillion, on his charger on the first stage of her journey to Burgundy, a growing estrangement between the King of England and his most powerful noble now seemed inevitable.

In the spring of 1469, Richard Neville, with his wife and his two daughters, Isabel and Anne, visited Duchess Margaret in Burgundy, had discussions on matters of state with her husband Charles, and then made a leisurely tour of the countryside, ending in Calais. Here Warwick could take his leisure with an old comrade, Sir John, now Lord, Wenlock, inspect the new fortifications, and check on progress with rebuilding of the fleet. His absence also ensured that he could not be associated with growing unrest in North Yorkshire, where one, Robert Huldyard, adopting the pseudonym "Robin of Redesdale", had raised the county and by May, was marching on York with 15,000 men, demanding redress of grievances.

This rising was quickly quelled by John Neville in his capacity of Warden of the Eastern Marches and Huldyard was executed in York. Warwick had returned from France and was constantly with the King during this time, reassuring him that his brother could keep the north quiet without reinforcement. However, a month later, "Robin of Redesdale" made a reappearance, the nom de guerre this time being taken by that veteran soldier Robert Ogle, who with Sir John Conyers and Henry Neville, Warwick's cousin and heir to Lord Latimer, led a well-armed force through South Yorkshire and onwards towards Nottingham, where King Edward awaited reinforcements from the southwest and from Wales. Contrary to the King's expectation, the Yorkshiremen did not lay siege to the city, but kept moving south and interposed between the King's small force and the approaching support led by William Herbert, newly installed Earl of Pembroke and Humphrey Stafford, equally new to his title of Earl of Devonshire. The two armies met at Edgecot on July 26th and the loyal forces were defeated in detail. Edward's own army dissolved on hearing this news and the King was taken and held captive by Warwick in his stronghold at Middleham.

While his northerners were moving towards the decisive confrontation, the Earl of Warwick had further strengthened his hand by re-crossing to Calais, where his elder daughter, Isabel, became wife to George of

Clarence, heir apparent to his brother, King Edward, on the 11th of July 1469. Returning immediately to England, Warwick took over the reins of power and with the apparently ready acquiescence of his royal captive effectively ruled England from his Wensleydale castle. Soon, however, Edward moved to Pontefract, so that his people might see that he was at full liberty to move around his realm and there, on October 6th, Richard of Gloucester, the King's youngest brother, with Lord Hastings, Edward's old comrade in arms, arrived, with an escort of 2,000 well-armed cavalry to convey the King back to his capital.

Immediately on his return to his seat of power, Edward rescinded virtually all of Warwick's appointments and restored his own men to the key positions of the Kingdom. John Neville, brother to the Kingmaker, who had demonstrated his own loyalty to Edward many times, was, nevertheless, stripped of the Earldom of Northumberland he had earned through victories against the King's enemies at Hedgley Moor and Hexham. Clearly, Edward had decided it was time to break the power of the Nevilles and Warwick moved quickly to buttress his failing authority in the land. In the spring of 1470, a new rebellion arose in Lincolnshire and Edward sent out commissions of array to all his Lords, including Warwick and Clarence, to raise their levies and meet with him and his army at Grantham on March 12th. Warwick sent word that he would do so but secretly instructed the leader of the rebels, Sir Robert Welles, to lead his forces to Leicester, by-passing the royal army and join there with him and Clarence, cutting Edward off from London.

This time, expecting treachery, Edward was not taken by surprise and caught Welles's army near the village of Empingham as they moved northwest from Stamford towards Melton Mowbray. There he destroyed the rebel force and when this news reached Warwick and his son-in-law, they fled by a circuitous route to Dartmouth and thence, with a hastily improvised fleet, the guilty pair reached Calais. Unhappily for them, royal orders had been sent to Wenlock that Warwick was not to be allowed to berth his ships there and the Kingmaker moved on to the Seine estuary, where Louis of France allowed him to take refuge at Honfleur and began to consider ways in which his old friend Richard Neville might be useful to the cause of France.

By the middle of June 1470, the Spider King's master plan was completed. Warwick and Margaret of Anjou would combine their powers in unholy alliance aimed at restoring Henry VI to his throne. The pauper-queen, her regal pride still intact, proved difficult to persuade that this was the only course left open to her, but eventually she agreed to the concord, and to its sealing by the marriage of her son to Warwick's younger daughter. However, she did impose two unalterable conditions. The mighty Earl of Warwick must make public apology to her on bended knee, in Angers and again in Westminster after King Henry's readeption, for the wrongs he had done her and her House, and neither she nor her son would return to England until all trace of Yorkist power had been eradicated.

With the degrading, but essential, preliminaries out of the way, Warwick sent word to his liegemen in North Yorkshire and Cumbria and by the beginning of August, Warwick's brother-in-law Henry Fitzhugh, his faithful Steward of Middleham John Conyers, and Richard Salkeld the Constable of Carlisle, had raised thousands of men who were mustering to march on York, where the real leader of the rising would soon appear – or so it seemed to King Edward. He raised the southern levies and, with Richard of Gloucester and Lords Hastings and Scales, he was at Ripon by August 14th. Such was his reputation for ruthless suppression of rebellion that the opposition seemed to melt before his army's approach and Edward was issuing pardons to repentant insurgents by the beginning of September, believing that all was well again. Then came the news that while the King was suppressing insurrection in the northland, Warwick had landed at the head of a small army of returned Lancastrians 300 miles away at Plymouth and Dartmouth on September 13th and supporters of the old regime were flocking to his standard.

Edward moved south to meet this threat but when he reached Doncaster, he learned that Warwick was now leading 30,000 men to meet him and John Neville, latterly Earl of Northumberland, refused to join the royal force with his Pontefract garrison. The King then realised he had no other course than to take flight out of the country and, on October 2nd, he and his brother Richard, with a few attendants took ship from Lynn in Norfolk for Burgundy. The Earl of Warwick's masterly strategy had given him the Kingdom of England with barely a blow struck and now he moved quickly to the seat of government in Westminster and the physical restoration of Henry VI to his throne. The reins of real power would remain, as Warwick had always intended, in his own hands.

Lady Margaret Beaufort, Countess of Richmond

(Detail from the w.w.w.)

CHAPTER FOURTEEN

A Game of Hide and Seek

On Saint Valentine's Day 1471, Edmund Beaufort, with his brother, John, returned to England and rode immediately towards the southwest in order to begin the recovery and, where necessary, the renovation of the family estates. He made no contact with the new ruler of the country, Richard Neville, but, en route, he called to pay his respects to the nominal head of the Beaufort dynasty, Margaret, Countess of Richmond, Lady Stafford, at her residence Woking Old Hall in Surrey. This first reunion of two returning exiles, men hardened by experience of war and the more-cruel blows of an unpredictable Fate, with a woman, small in stature but with the same burning Beaufort ambition clearly apparent, was brief. However, it was renewed again in the early days of spring, when Somerset and his brother returned to the Hall, following news of King Edward's landing at Ravenspur in Yorkshire.

The Beauforts were raising men to resist the Yorkist resurgence and urged Stafford to bring his retainers and join with them. Henry Stafford had fought with Lancaster's beaten army at Towton and had made his peace with Edward immediately afterwards. He and his wife could see no purpose in forsaking their ten-year allegiance to York without lengthier consideration and, four days later, Somerset left his relatives with nothing more than promises of continued contact and further consideration of his call to arms. When parting, Stafford asked where and when he intended to join forces with the Earl of Warwick, but Somerset evaded a direct reply and suggested Stafford keep in touch with him at his headquarters in Salisbury. It was clear to the Staffords that their unruly cousin intended to concentrate his efforts in the southwest of the country, where he expected to greet Queen Margaret and her son as soon as they came ashore to reclaim their realm and, meantime, he would await the outcome of the coming confrontation between the Nevilles and the House of York.

Henry Stafford was less fortunate in the last respect. Edward IV arrived in London with a growing army on April 11th and summoned all his retainers and nobles to rally to him there. Stafford, feeling the balance of power had moved towards the Yorkist King, joined Edward's army and marched with it to Barnet three days later. Here, in the swirling mists and confusion that marked the last fight of Richard of Warwick and John Neville, former Earl of Northumberland, Henry Stafford received serious wounds, which, despite the devoted ministrations of his wife, Margaret Beaufort, would prove mortal and lead to his death in the early days of October.

Margaret of Anjou, titular Queen of England since her marriage to Henry VI in 1445, landed at Weymouth in the early evening of Easter Day, April 14th 1471. With her came John, Lord Wenlock, erstwhile Captain of Calais, Sir John Langstrother, Prior of the Order of Hospitallers, with many other knights and gentlemen, and her only child, Edward of Lancaster, Prince of Wales with his new wife, Anne Neville. Margaret was greeted by Edmund Beaufort and asked him how the Earl of Warwick's campaign against the usurper, Edward, was progressing. Somerset said he awaited news from London, which was expected shortly and with this, Margaret had to be content.

However, next day messengers riding sweat-lathered horses arrived to report the evil fate which had befallen Lancaster's hopes at Barnet and the Queen pondered the advisability of an immediate return to the safe haven of France. Somerset dissuaded her from such a course, since he and the Earl of Devon had already recruited a substantial force and more would come in as they moved northwards through Exeter towards the Severn crossing. There they could expect to meet Jasper Tudor with thousands of Welsh at his back and together they could move on the capital for a final accounting with Edward of York. Unwilling to return to the penury she had endured for so long, Margaret agreed to stay in England and to renew the struggle to restore her husband's throne and her son's inheritance.

Triumphantly Edmund Beaufort, the Queen and the Prince of Wales riding with him, led his forces westwards towards Exeter. Now the world should see that there was another trained fighting man in England, who could match the war-skills and experience of the usurping Edward. The fortunes of Lancaster would burgeon again, with its bastard sprig, the House of Beaufort, playing a valiant and rewarding role in the restoration of the rightful rulers of England.

Somerset moved his growing army steadily north from Exeter, gathering men and materiel along the way, with a strong screen of scouts out to cover his eastern flank, whence any attack from Edward would come. By the end of April, he had reached Bath without interference and with no indication that any hostile force was in his vicinity. He therefore moved the six miles west to Bristol, where further reinforcements and provisions awaited collection and rested his troops there on the first night of May. Unhappily, his sleep was broken by riders from the screen of scouts with news of a great host which had arrived at Malmesbury and was therefore in a position to interpose between Somerset and his immediate objective of the Severn crossing at Gloucester, when he resumed his march at sunrise.

Beaufort had learned the value of acting speedily on intelligence brought in by scouts and, without wasting time, he roused his camp and marched eastwards, as though to meet Edward. Short of Sodbury, he swung north again towards Gloucester, but, having located the enemy, he left a strong force of cavalry to act as rearguard and, at need, to delay any pursuers. This screening force moved into Sodbury at first light, where they ran headlong into scouts sent out by Edward to locate Lancaster's army. They captured a number of these and learning from them that the King was still unaware of the location and line of march of their main force, they spurred on after Somerset to tell him the good tidings.

Surviving scouts raced back to Edward with the intelligence that they had run into the vanguard of Somerset's army and he quickened his march accordingly down the road from Malmesbury, reaching Sodbury Hill about mid-morning. Here he arrayed his army for battle and awaited the approach of the oncoming Lancastrians. When nothing had happened as the evening shadows closed in, he decided to hold the bulk of his force in its naturally strong position, but sent out riders south, west and north, with instructions to find the enemy. He was awakened at three o clock in the morning of May 3rd with the news that Somerset and his army were 14 miles north of him and already on the final leg of their march to Gloucester.

Having slipped past Edward at Sodbury, Somerset had made the best of his way towards Berkeley, a march of well over 20 miles which had been completed in just over 14 hours. Reaching the town at twilight and with only 14 miles further to go to Gloucester, the Lancastrian commander decided to rest his men for a few hours and make an early start for his immediate destination. Shortly after midnight, the sergeants and knights roused the army again and set out on the last lap of their race for the crossing of the Severn, which would lead to safe haven with Jasper Tudor, and his horde of Welshmen. They reached the town by mid-morning and there they found the gates barred against them. Edward's army was still miles behind, but fast-riding heralds had carried orders to Richard Beauchamp, Governor of Gloucester, that at all costs he must hold the town for York and Beauchamp, as Edward knew, was a loyal and resolute man.

Edmund Beaufort summoned Beauchamp to open the gates to his Queen and her army so they might pass over the bridge, which the town's defences commanded. The Governor, faithful to his salt, refused, even though he was terrified by the size of Lancaster's army and subjected to a barrage of abuse and threats of dire consequences if the gates were not thrown open at once. Beaufort, when bluff and bluster were clearly not enough to make Beauchamp give way, briefly considered trying to storm the walls and force his way over the bridge, but knew that Edward must be in hot pursuit by this time and dared not risk being caught between two enemy forces. The Queen was adamant that the army must link with Tudor's force before facing Edward in full-scale battle and Somerset had no option but to order the army to continue its march northwards.

Ten miles further along the road, the Lancastrians came to Tewkesbury, a pretty market town surrounded by rich farmland. Here a crossing of the Severn was possible and there was no opposition to this from within the unwalled township, but Somerset knew Edward would be on his heels and could not take the chance of being caught with half his army strung out making the crossing. He therefore deployed his weary men in a defensive line across a low ridge lying south of the town, which covered both approach roads, and settled there for the night with the intention of making an early crossing, if he could do so before the Yorkists came up with him.

His hope was vain. Having realised that Somerset had, literally, stolen a march on him, Edward had driven his army relentlessly over 30 miles to Cheltenham. Then, after scouts had brought back news of Beauchamp's successful resistance, he roused the worn-out men again and drove them on four miles more to a village called Tredington, which lay barely three miles short of Somerset's lines. Now there could be no further retreat. Now Lancaster must fight and win, if its army was to link with the allied force in

Wales. Now Edmund Beaufort must prove he was the better general, the fiercer warrior, or perish in the attempt. Both sides settled to get what rest they could before the inevitable conflict began. It was the night of May 3rd 1471.

Coat of Arms of Lady Margaret Beaufort.

(Detail from the w.w.w.)

CHAPTER FIFTEEN

"And he that will not fight for such a hope,
Go home to bed and, like the owl by day,
If he arise, be mock'd and wond'red at..."
[Henry VI Pt 3]

In the early light of the following morning, Beaufort studied the ground in front of the right wing of the army, where his own division was formed for battle. Immediately in front of him was a low, flat-topped hillock with, further still to the right, a patch of woodland. He had noted the features when arraying his men, the evening before and the germ of an idea had come to him. As he looked at the ground again, now, in the light of day, he felt certain that the manoeuvre he had in mind would destroy Edward's army and, excited by the prospect of final Lancastrian victory, he sent for his brother John and for Lord Wenlock, who, with the Prince of Wales, commanded the centre division.

Together the three men rode forward to check the area around the hillock and found that there was sufficient space there for a large body of men to move round the far side, out of sight of the enemy force, and to take the opposing left flank by surprise. The charge would either roll up the opposing division and break it, or cause it to wheel and face the attack, in which event it must expose its right flank to the Lancastrian centre. Were this to happen, Wenlock must immediately charge home and, between the two forces, a third of Edward's army would be destroyed and the rest could be driven from the field. Since Edward had never fled any battle, he would be taken and receive short shrift in the bloody aftermath. Satisfied with the viability of his plan and that Wenlock understood his part in the scheme, Somerset rode back briskly to his lines to enjoy a hearty breakfast. He might have eaten less well had he known that his was not the only early-morning reconnaissance of the field.

Edward IV, with Richard of Gloucester and William, Lord Hastings, had ridden forward from Tredington to survey the ground over which he would fight. He noted that Lancaster's line was well protected, particularly in the centre, by broken ground, sunken lanes, ditches and hedges, which must hamper any approach. The enemy's right flank, where Somerset's banners waved, looked more approachable and Edward resolved he would make his first attack there with his brother Richard's vanguard, which had acquitted itself so well at Barnet, three weeks before. This would require a change in the usual method of arraying an army, where the column of march, on reaching the battleground, would invariably swing to the right and thus form the right wing of the eventual line. At Tewkesbury, Richard would lead the host on to the field, but would wheel his division in the opposite direction and command the left flank, with Edward taking his customary position in the centre and Hastings on the right.

Studying the enemy's array and the ground in front for a last time before riding back to dispose his approaching army, Edward noted the wooded area beyond the hillock to Somerset's front. If the enemy commander had thoughts of any kind of clever manoeuvre, that would be the place to try it, perhaps by infiltrating men through the woods, attacking his baggage trains behind the main army, causing pandemonium and confusion generally. He would guard against any surprise there by infiltrating a flank guard of 200 lances, who could warn of the approach of any substantial enemy force seeking to outflank the Yorkist army. Satisfied with the planned disposition of his army, Edward rode back toward Tredington to hasten his men forward.

About mid-morning, Somerset watched as the Yorkist army reached the field and saw Gloucester lead his men in a wheel to the left and deploy opposite the section of his line where the Beaufort banners flaunted in the breeze. The bulk of his division, however, was already in place hidden behind the hillock and waiting his command. Only a skeleton force waved spears and shouted from behind the hedge and it was towards this target that Richard of Gloucester directed his advance on his brother's signal. Struggling to keep their dressing over the rough ground, Gloucester's men reached a point opposite the hillock and were suddenly taken in the flank by Somerset's furious charge. Thrown into momentary confusion, the troops rallied to their leader's commands and gradually swung to their left to face the onslaught. Slowly but surely they reformed their ranks until they were fighting Edmund Beaufort's division along a line at right angles to their original track and while they were holding their opponents, their manoeuvre had separated them from their centre, leaving their right flank in the air at the mercy of Wenlock's men.

TEWKESBURY. May 4th 1471.

Beaufort's plan had worked to perfection. Gloucester and his division would be crushed by the second flank attack from Wenlock and the battle was as good as over. Lancaster would triumph and the Duke of Somerset would emerge from Tewkesbury field as England's greatest general. If only Wenlock would attack, and time and again Somerset looked to his left and ordered trumpets to call the centre of his line into the action. But still Wenlock sat in the centre of his division, with Edward of Lancaster, Prince of Wales beside him and did not move.

The flank guard which Edward had stationed in the woods beyond the hillock to warn of any enemy approach from that direction had searched their area thoroughly and found nothing. They could hear the roar of battle to their right and, when this seemed to be mounting, they rode to the edge of the trees nearest the action to observe events obviously much more exciting than their own mundane duty of keeping a sharp lookout. And there, to their astonished gaze was revealed the rear and right flank of Edmund Beaufort's division, locked in battle with Gloucester's wing. Unlike Wenlock, without more ado, they lowered their lance points and charged.

Beaufort's troops staggered under the impact of the lancers' assault and now under attack from front, flank and rear, his line began to unravel. He tried desperately to rally the men, but it was of no use. Gloucester had sensed the shock and the fear which had run through the force opposite and redoubled his own efforts to force the enemy line back. It was too much, the Lancastrians broke and ran. Somerset, maddened with disappointment, hot-blooded still from the fight, galloped back to the centre of his battle-line, where Wenlock waited still with the Prince, his bare head evidence of his unreadiness to join in the fight, his expression impassive in face of Lancaster's imminent, disastrous defeat. Edmund Beaufort raised his battleaxe and clove Wenlock's skull to the chine.

Edward's centre division had reached the hedge at last and, with Gloucester's wing coming round the open flank and the King's fresh troops charging triumphantly in the front, Somerset saw his army turn to flee and rode his weary horse up the meadow to the Abbey, where, with many others in the last stages of exhaustion, he claimed sanctuary. They did not see the destruction of their remaining force under John Courtenay, titular Earl of Devon, nor the pursuit of their fugitives across the fields towards the barrier of the Severn, which became a killing ground known ever after as Bloody

Meadow, but they knew their course was run.

Suddenly, there were shouts from the Abbey doorway, armour clashing, heavy footsteps echoing in the lofty roof and the giant, steel-covered figure of Edward IV strode into the hallowed precincts, sword in hand, determined to make an end of Lancaster once and for all. Bravely, the Father Abbot stood before his King and pleaded for the lives of the men who had sought temporary safety there; amidst the throng, remnants of his tattered surcoat hidden, Somerset watched and waited Edward's decision. The King hesitated, then bowed and turned away, ordering his men to leave this Holy place without harm to those it sheltered. Vastly relieved, the weary beaten men of Lancaster settled down to rest, tend their hurts, count their missing and name their dead.

Their respite was brief indeed. In the morning they were asked to leave the Abbey, the King having given assurances for their safety. When the refugees emerged, blinking, into the sunlight, Edmund Beaufort and Sir John Langstrother, Prior of the Hospitallers, with various other knights known as long-term supporters of the Lancastrian cause, were taken aside while the majority of the captives were allowed to disperse after renewing their fealty to King Edward. Then, the principal captives were given time to make their peace with God and quickly despatched by the headsman. In death, they rejoined Edward of Lancaster, Prince of Wales and only heir of Henry VI, Courtenay of Devon, John Beaufort, self-styled Marquess of Dorset and many knights and gentlemen who had been killed in battle or in fleeing from the stricken field.

With the death of Edmund Beaufort, typical of his strain, handsome, brash, vain – a better war-chief than most of his forebears, but no match for the greatest King-general England would ever produce – the male line directly descended from John of Gaunt was extinguished. But still the family's unending quest for ultimate power would continue through its titular head, a diminutive, sharp-featured woman with hooded eyes, Margaret Beaufort, only child of John, first Duke of Somerset, who in her turn also had a single child, a boy called Henry Tudor.

Execution of Edmund Beaufort, 4th Duke of Somerset.

(G. Wheeler)

Part Five

The Last of the Beauforts

CHAPTER SIXTEEN

A Much Married Lady

Margaret Beaufort, Countess of Richmond, was the great survivor of her family and, indeed, of her time. She was born on May 31st 1443, and the first of her four marriages took place six years later. Her childhood spouse was John de la Pole, who would become second Duke of Suffolk following his father, the ill-fated William, who rose high in the counsels of his King, Henry VI, stood proxy for him at his wedding to the proud Princess, Margaret of Anjou, and died by the stroke of a rusty sword on Dover beach in the spring of 1450. Margaret's marriage into the de la Pole family was annulled two years after Suffolk's death and the arranging of her future nuptial vows was taken in hand by the King himself. On November 1st 1455, she re-married, this time with Edmund, Earl of Richmond, who was the elder son of Katherine of France and her Gentleman of the Bedchamber, Owen Tudor, and, thereby, half-brother to King Henry.

Marriage to one of the richest heiresses in England was an enormous stroke of luck for the comparatively poorly-off Richmond and he lost no time in consummating the match. Their first, and Margaret's only, child was born on January 28th 1457, before the Countess had celebrated her fourteenth birthday, a boy who was christened Henry, after his royal uncle. Edmund Tudor never saw his son having died of the plague on November 3rd 1456 and his widow, with her brother-in-law, Jasper, Earl of Pembroke, travelled to Greenfield Manor, near Newport in the early spring of 1457 to arrange her third marriage to Henry Stafford, younger son of the first Duke of Buckingham. This union was cemented at the beginning of January in 1458 and would last for close on 14 years.

Henry, Lord Stafford, like all his forebears, was a loyal Lancastrian and fought on the losing side at Towton. Having survived that awful carnage on Palm Sunday 1461, Stafford made his submission to the Yorkist King, Edward IV, and continued loyal to his oath until his death. On his wife's urging, he regularly wrote to his new royal master, pressing his step-son's right to the title and lands of Richmond, but without a great deal of success. Nevertheless, he rode from his stately home in Surrey to follow Edward IV to Barnet, where he was severely wounded and would die in the October following, leaving his thrice widowed relict, still only 28 years old, to consider whether or no to undertake a further matrimonial alliance.

Before Stafford reached the end of his mortal coil, however, Margaret Beaufort had to deal with a matter of even greater urgency: the safety of her son, Henry Tudor. The boy, now past his fifteenth birthday, had been staying in Wales with his uncle Jasper, who had returned home following Warwick's brief restoration of Henry VI, and had been gathering men in the Principality to support Margaret of Anjou and Edmund Beaufort against King Edward. After Lancaster's hopes of restoration were finally and irrevocably shattered at Tewkesbury, and Henry VI's life was ended in the Tower on May 21st, it would clearly have been foolish in the extreme for Jasper Tudor to remain within Edward's reach and he set sail for France on June 2nd, landing finally in Brittany, where Duke Francis gave him refuge. At his mother's bidding, Henry Tudor went with him, thus avoiding being caught in King Edward's clean sweep of his enemies – actual and potential – as a possible pretender to the crown of England. With her heir and "England's Hope", as Henry VI allegedly referred to the young Tudor, safely harboured out of Edward's immediate reach, Margaret Beaufort turned again to thoughts of possible re-marriage.

This time, her eventual choice lighted on Thomas, Lord Stanley, a widower, formerly married to Eleanor Neville, sister of Warwick the Kingmaker, whose extensive land holdings in Lancashire, Cheshire and the northwest fitted well with her own in the southern counties and in the Midlands. A formal agreement was drawn up under which Stanley got a life interest in her land holdings and she drew an annual income of 500 marks from his estates. Lord Stanley was probably the greatest side-changer in the wars which had beset England for the previous 16 years and seemed to have a God-given facility for always being found, ultimately, coupled with the victors. He had also linked with the Queen's family through the marriage of his son George, Lord Strange, with Jacquetta Woodville, Elizabeth's sister, and Margaret Beaufort took pains to strengthen this bond. The success of her endeavours was evidenced seven years later, when she was chosen to carry Princess Bridget, the last child to be born to Edward IV, to her christening.

At no time during her lengthy period of strengthening her family's links with the House of Edward of York, did Margaret Beaufort forget her direct descent from Edward III, nor her position as the effective leader of what was left of Lancaster and all that this implied for the future fortune of her son. He, the Countess of Richmond was certain, would one day sit on England's throne as Henry VII, the first of the Tudor dynasty and the last of the Beauforts. She kept in constant touch with him during his exile in Brittany, mainly through the intermediacy of her faithful steward who had transferred his total loyalty to her after the death of Henry Stafford. He was a large, strong, crude man called Reginald Bray, who had a great facility for anonymity, which would stand him, and Margaret Beaufort, in good stead during years to come.

On April 9th 1483, the life of Edward IV ended peacefully in his bed and the Countess of Richmond knew that his widow, Elizabeth Woodville, with the assistance of her family, would set in motion the plans they had made. These entailed bringing the new King, Edward V, quickly to London, a speedy coronation, and the inception of a Regency Council, which, under Queen Elizabeth as regent, would rule England. The need for haste lay in the absence in the north of the King's brother, Richard, Duke of Gloucester, who, according to a codicil to the late King's will would be installed as Protector and take on the supervision and guidance of his nephew during his minority. With the new King already crowned, the Office of Protector automatically ceased and Gloucester would exercise no power in the realm, other than that given to him by the King and his Council of Regency.

Lord Stanley and his wife knew of the plot through Stanley's membership of the Council, where Edward's stepson, Thomas Grey, Marquess of Dorset, had taken on himself considerable authority and regularly pressed his fellow members to support the Woodvilles' policy line. They had also received confidential approaches from the Queen, asking them for their support, but confined themselves to positive-sounding responses rather than actual promises. The prudence of the Stanleys' reception of Woodville blandishments became evident when, in the late evening of the last day of April, hard-riding couriers from Stony Stratford reached Westminster

Elizabeth Woodville, Queen of England.

(Detail from the Royal Window, Canterbury Cathedral)

140

bearing news of the arrests of the Queen's brother, Anthony Woodville, Earl Rivers, with her son, Lord Richard Grey and sundry courtiers, by the Duke of Gloucester supported by Henry Stafford, Duke of Buckingham. The two Dukes would continue on to London, escorting King Edward in stately procession, and were expected to reach the capital on Sunday, May 4th.

The support for the Woodville family in Council and among the nobles of the court melted like summer snow at the news. The Queen and Dorset moved, with much of the late King's treasure, into sanctuary at Westminster Abbey; Sir Edward Woodville, High Admiral and a leading supporter of his sister's plotting, had already put to sea, with his fleet and his share of the royal treasury. The Chancellor of England and Archbishop of York, Thomas Rotherham, sent the Great Seal to the Queen for safe-keeping, then thought it better to retain it pending the Protector's arrival and asked for it back. And, amidst all the cowardice, panic and general apprehension, four of those who, in one way or another, had been involved in recent events, kept their heads.

They were William Hastings, the Lord Chamberlain, who had sent messengers to tell Gloucester of his brother's death; John Morton, Bishop of Ely, for years a trusted councillor of Edward IV and loyal to Lancaster throughout his long life; Thomas, Lord Stanley, who had constantly appeared on the winning side through all the undulations of fate over the previous 30 years, and his wife, Lady Margaret, head of the House of Beaufort, who was beginning to wonder how best the recent transformations might be used to the benefit of herself and her son.

Now within days of her fortieth birthday, Margaret Beaufort took stock of her resources. With Elizabeth Woodville reduced to the status of queen-mother, the Countess of Richmond had become the wealthiest woman in England. Her marriage to Henry Stafford had made her persona grata to the ruling House of York, an advantage reinforced by her subsequent espousal of Thomas Stanley. The Stanleys, like Margaret Beaufort herself, were great survivors of the wars between the Plantagenets and Lord Thomas bid fair to be the greatest trimmer of them all. He took little or no active part in battles fought during the earlier years of conflict. Following a skirmish between some of his men and Richard of Gloucester's troops, he had chosen to ignore his brother-in-law's pleas for help, when the Kingmaker and Clarence were searching desperately for allies after Empingham, yet was able to reach an early accommodation with Richard Neville during the brief readeption.

As Edward IV landed at Ravenspur in mid-March 1471 to reclaim his crown, Thomas Stanley was busy besieging Hornby Castle, in pursuit of his own family's feud with the Harringtons. He was, therefore, too busy to join Warwick before Barnet, or Somerset at Tewkesbury, but not too preoccupied with personal affairs to miss welcoming the victorious Yorkist leader back to his rightful place on the throne. Soon Lord Thomas would become Steward of the Royal Household and acquire numerous posts of influence and profit in the northwest, where he was seen as one of the bastions of Edward's rule. He was in a position to be of enormous help to his wife in her scheme to ensure that her son, Henry Tudor, last of the Beauforts, sat one day in his rightful place on the throne of England.

Another, who could help her cause in different ways, was one of the few persons Margaret had met, who could match her own intellect. He was the Bishop of Ely, John Morton, who had likewise made his peace with Edward IV after Tewkesbury and then had worked his way up through the echelons of the Civil Service until he had a rich bishopric, the friendship of the Queen and her family, an appointment to instruct the Prince of Wales in kingly virtues, and a place in the King's Council where he discussed the great decisions of State with the mightiest Lords of the land. And, as Margaret Beaufort knew well, Morton's innermost loyalties were still to the lost cause of Lancaster and would be easily transferred to her son as the last of the bloodline. John Morton would indeed be an invaluable asset.

Finally, and unexpectedly, it seemed there was her nephew by marriage and cousin by blood, Henry Stafford, second Duke of Buckingham. Harry Buckingham was now 30, descended directly from Edward III on his father's side and from John of Gaunt through his Beaufort mother, and the greatest responsibility Edward IV had seen fit to give him was the occasion five years earlier when he was selected to pass the formal sentence of death on the King's brother George, Duke of Clarence. Married, unwillingly, at 13 years of age to Katherine Woodville, the Queen's sister, Henry Stafford had cordially loathed all Woodvilles ever after and they, for their part, had seen to it that the career of the ebullient Buckingham, who had the Plantagenet temper in full measure, was confined to the fringes of court affairs. And now, with the world again turned upside down, the overweight, effete, febrile dandy had become brother-in-arms to Richard, Duke of Gloucester, the greatest man in England after the King. Lady Stanley must assuredly develop her hitherto rather tenuous links with her nephew. Who could tell what might not come out of that?

Having mentally catalogued the help available for her efforts in behalf of her son, Margaret Beaufort turned to thoughts of the obstacles to Henry achieving the crown which should be his. This list was much shorter than the first. The highest-placed, immediate stumbling blocks were the young, new King, Edward V, whose coronation was to take place in the month following his arrival in London, and his still younger brother, Richard, Duke of York. After them would come the Duke of Gloucester, Lord Protector of the realm and that other surviving pillar of the House of York, William, Lord Hastings. Then, there could be peripheral difficulties caused by the Woodville clique, but she felt these could be dealt with quite easily, through her long-standing project of a marriage between Henry Tudor and Elizabeth of York, Edward IV's eldest child.

The cast of the drama chose itself; the principal players were discerned. Now, it was simply a matter of awaiting developments and seeing what might be done, by whom and to whom, to help the business on.

Seal of Lady Margaret Beaufort

(G. Wheeler)

Henry Stafford.
2nd Duke of Buckingham

(Engraving taken from a traditional portrait)

CHAPTER SEVENTEEN

"Ay, now the plot thickens very much upon us..."
[George Villiers, Duke of Buckingham]

The royal procession, led by Edward V supported by his uncle, Richard of Gloucester and his distant cousin, Henry of Buckingham, reached London in the morning of the first Sunday in May 1483 and processed through cheering crowds and ringing bells to St Paul's and on to the Palace of the Bishop of London, where the young King was lodged. Immediately thereafter, Gloucester sent calls to all Officers and Councillors to meetings at which arrangements for the government of the land and the formal crowning of its new King would be discussed and agreed. He made few changes in existing appointments. The Great Seal and the Office of Chancellor was transferred to the more stable grasp of John Russell, Bishop of Lincoln and a cleric who had served Edward IV well over the years. Thomas Rotherham was allowed to keep his place on the Council, as were most of the existing members, including Thomas Stanley and John Morton, with Henry Stafford being added to their ranks, and William Hastings was confirmed in his Offices of Lord Chamberlain and Captain of Calais.

With the essential appointments settled, the Council decided June 24th would be the new date for Edward's Coronation and the King was moved from the Bishop's Palace to the royal apartments in the Tower, still the most secure fortress in England. The continued detention of Earl Rivers, his nephew Richard Grey and the King's former tutor Thomas Vaughan, was agreed, pending further examination, and the Queen's brother, Edward Woodville and her eldest son, Thomas Grey, were declared outlaws and a price put on their heads. The decisions coming out of Council under the new regime were perfectly in harmony with the views expressed by William Hastings, which was appropriate to his length of service, experience in government and his leadership of the "greybeard" group advising the Protector: Stanley, Rotherham, Morton and the rest. The only imperfection in the revised arrangement from Hastings' standpoint was the apparent importance attached by Richard of Gloucester to the views expressed, with increasing frequency, by the Duke of Buckingham. Lord Hastings placed little value on the opinions of one new to the great councils of the land, who had never imperilled life and estates in the service of the House of York and he made no secret of his growing dislike of the young incomer to the other old hands.

All of this, Stanley and Morton reported to and discussed with Margaret Beaufort and the three agreed that here was a potential cause for tension between the Protector and his brother's oldest friend, through which the governance of the kingdom might be disrupted to the benefit of the Lancastrian cause. The men would encourage Hastings' jealousy of the new man and Lady Margaret would similarly influence her nephew against the late King's best friend. Between the three, much useful mischief might be conjured.

In addition to cultivating a closer relationship with her nephew, Lady Stanley took pains to maintain her well-established links with Elizabeth Woodville and her daughters whom the Queen had taken with her into sanctuary. The Beaufort family physician, Lewis, was sent to minister to any minor ailments the unhappy family contracted and often Margaret Beaufort herself would visit them, bringing small comforts of food and wine. She also brought news of events outside the Abbey and spent hours discussing with the Queen plans which, it was rumoured, the Protector was making to usurp the crown. These were being countered by the efforts of loyal members of the Council, but they could only use delaying tactics and more effective means would be necessary, if Edward's right to succeed were to be safeguarded.

The royal ladies easily agreed on the right man to lead opposition to the Duke of Gloucester's designs. Lord Hastings was well known in court and country, he was the late King's best friend and comrade-in-arms and was wealthy and powerful in his own right. It was true he had little affection for the Woodville family, witness his recent, and successful, efforts to forestall their coup d'etat, but proposals might be made to him via Lord Stanley, which could be supported by the Queen's good friend, the Bishop of Ely, and it would be useful if Jane Shore, with whom Elizabeth Woodville had always had good relations, could supplement the persuasion of Hastings through "pillow talk" with her new lover. Then, once the desired results had been achieved with Edward V crowned and his mother installed as Regent, further changes might be made in arrangements with Lord Hastings, as circumstances demanded.

In the days following, both ladies played their parts, as did Stanley and John Morton and an important additional member joined the alliance. Henry Stafford, Duke of Buckingham, was easily angered by hints, then assertions, of Hastings' dislike for him and reports of his secret plots to bring down the Protector and Buckingham with him, and was dissuaded only with difficulty from rushing to Richard with news of the treason that was planned. In short space, this new, powerful weapon was primed and waiting only the spark to fire the fuse, when Fate intervened to seal Hastings' doom.

Robert Stillington, Bishop of Bath and Wells and one-time Chancellor of England, had called on Richard of Gloucester secretly and told him that his brother's marriage to Elizabeth Woodville had been bigamous. A pre-contract of marriage had existed with Lady Eleanor Butler, daughter of John Talbot, Earl of Shrewsbury, when Edward took his Queen to wife, and this had never been annulled. The children of the following union were bastards, and there could never be any question of young Edward sitting in his father's place. Richard had confided in Buckingham and he, in turn, could hardly wait to share, with his friends and family, this marvellous revelation spelling the final downfall of the hated Woodvilles' power in the land. With the added rider that, until Richard decided on the appropriate course he must now take, all must be kept a closely guarded secret.

The Stanleys and Morton agreed entirely with Buckingham's request for silence and assured him of their support for any course of action ultimately decided by the Lord Protector. Then, Hastings was advised of developments and immediate action urged to prevent what was obviously a pretext on Gloucester's part to usurp the crown. He swallowed the alternative interpretation of events whole and, further, willingly accepted the leading role in a counterplot concocted by Morton, which must end in the arrest or, if necessary, the assassination of the Protector. The coup was timed for the next meeting of Council and details of the scheme were immediately conveyed to Richard through the link with Buckingham.

The three conspirators now waited on events. How ever things turned out, one of the two main props of the House of York would be destroyed, which could only improve the prospects for Henry Tudor, last hope of the Beaufort line. Then further plans could be made in light of the outcome of the confrontation between Gloucester and Hastings.

On Friday, June 13th 1483 at 10 o' clock, a small, select number from the Council met in the White Tower and Hastings found himself hoist with his own petard. His men had been quietly detained before the meeting and it was the Protector's guards who rushed into the chamber in answer to his signal. The old courtier's guilt was made plain by his actions and Richard, enraged by the revelation of an assassination plot framed against him by an old and trusted comrade, dealt out summary justice there and then. Hastings was taken out and beheaded over a baulk of timber left outside the Tower by workmen; Rotherham was sent to other accommodation in the Tower while Richard considered how best to deal with him; Stanley went home, having received a slight head wound in the brief melee, which would be dressed by his wife while he related the success of their plans, and, at Buckingham's request, John Morton was banished to Brecknock, where the Duke vowed he would be kept secure.

Hastings' death caused a quickening in the pace of events. On June 25th, the Lords and Commons of England met together at Westminster, where they had been summoned to greet their new King, Edward V. Instead, they were told that his succession was rendered out of the question, through the bigamous nature of his mother's marriage to Edward IV. On the following day, the whole Parliament processed to Baynard's Castle, where Richard of Gloucester was lodged with his mother, Cecily, Duchess of York, and Buckingham acting as spokesman formally petitioned Richard "to take upon you the said crown and Royal Dignity". With obvious reluctance, Gloucester said he would act in accordance with their wishes and the assembly hailed him with great shouts of "Long live King Richard".

Some days before this momentous event, in pursuance of an earlier decision by the Council, Richard Ratcliffe had ridden north to Pomfret Castle with a warrant for the execution of Earl Rivers, Lord Richard Grey and Sir Thomas Vaughan, who had been brought together at Pontefract. Their sentence followed from the discovered involvement of Elizabeth Woodville

Richard III

(Original portrait by Ralph Taylor)

and Thomas Grey in Hastings' plot, and on June 25th the three men were beheaded in the presence of Henry Percy, Earl of Northumberland, the King's Warden for the northeast. News of their demise was carried back to London by Ratcliffe and added further to the tales of woe heaping upon Elizabeth Woodville in the sanctuary of Westminster Abbey. Her world had indeed turned upside down.

Lady Margaret Beaufort, on the other hand, inwardly rejoiced in the constant improvement, as she saw it, in her son's prospects of succession to the crown. Her husband, and she with him, stood high in the regard of the new King and her nephew, Buckingham, had emerged as the Monarch's strong right-hand. All this was clearly evidenced by the prestigious involvement of the three in the magnificent ceremony and subsequent celebration of Richard's coronation, which took place on July 6th 1483, and which would be followed by a grand tour of his new realm by the King. Henry Stafford would not immediately accompany Richard on his journey. He had left his Welsh estates three months before to join forces with the Duke of Gloucester, and had received additional lands in the coronation honours, all of which demanded his temporary presence at Brecknock Castle. Lord Stanley rode in the King's train, but his wife stayed at their London residence, from where she wrote to her son in France and to John Morton in his comfortable confinement at Brecknock.

With the King away from his capital for close on three months, Margaret Beaufort felt the time had come to implement her scheme for the final downfall of the House of York. She had maintained her connection with Elizabeth Woodville and had persuaded her that her family's fortunes might yet be restored by an alliance with the Beaufort interest, through the betrothal of Henry Tudor with Elizabeth of York, eldest child of Edward IV, which would be implemented on the downfall of Richard III. She knew, through correspondence with her son, that he hoped to bring an army to invade England in the autumn of the year, which would be reinforced by Woodville adherents and by the Lancastrian rump, of which Lady Stanley was the titular head. The final facet in her grand design, in the construction of which she had been greatly assisted by John Morton, was to bring about a rift between the King and Buckingham and the method they had agreed would, incidentally, remove a further, possible obstacle to her son's accession to the throne.

Morton, the cleverest and most experienced civil servant in the land, had seen clearly that, for a union between Henry Tudor and Elizabeth of York to add weight to the Tudor claim, it would be essential for the bride's natal legitimacy to be restored. However, such a process must also reinstate her brothers' right to the crown and their elimination from the scene therefore became a prerequisite for the success of the Beaufort plan. Fortuitously, this essential requirement could, simultaneously, provide the means to forging an irreparable estrangement between Richard III and his strongest supporter, thanks to the long-nurtured hatred harboured by Buckingham for the Woodville family and to the sway Morton had achieved over the Duke's mind. Margaret Beaufort, intent only on removing all barriers from her son's road to the crown, had agreed Morton's reasoning, urging only that whatever were done must be carried out while the King was distant from the main levers of his power, with which, Morton in his turn had agreed.

The outcome of this wicked correspondence was the secret killing of Edward V and his brother Richard, after removal from their apartments in the Tower on Buckingham's authority as Constable of England. The deed done, Buckingham – acting still on Morton's advice – had rushed after the King's progress to reveal his act of ultimate loyalty to his royal master and completely failed to understand the horrified abhorrence and rage his report engendered in a King whose loyalty to his dead brother and that brother's family had never been in doubt. Sent packing to Brecknock from Richard's presence, to await judgement after the essential tour had been completed, and little doubting what his sentence would be, an enraged and frightened Buckingham was easy prey for the clever nuances of thought of John Morton. Within days, he was actively planning his own leadership of the coming rebellion to unseat King Richard and to replace him with Henry Tudor. Only in this way, the Bishop had persuaded him, could he now protect his high position and keep his very life.

CHAPTER EIGHTEEN

"How now, Lord Stanley! What's the news? "

[Richard III]

Margaret Beaufort heard from Morton of the removal of the lesser obstacles in Henry Tudor's path to the throne. As Polydore Vergil would record, years later: "She, being a wise woman, after the slaughter of King Edward's children was known, began to hope well of her son's fortune" and she continued to liaise with Elizabeth Woodville, directly and through her physician, Lewis. By this means, the Queen was advised of Buckingham's change of heart – though not the real reason for it – and continued her efforts to revive supporters of the Woodville family, against the day when the whole country would rise in revolt against the usurper. Meanwhile, Lady Margaret had agreed with her husband's suggestion that it would be best to keep a foot in both camps and he would, therefore, not play an active role in the conspiracy, but, obviously, would bring his Cheshire legions to join the final battle on Tudor's side.

Throughout September, as the King progressed around his realm, Margaret Beaufort maintained an intense, clandestine correspondence with old supporters of Lancaster still in England, with her nephew, Henry of Buckingham, and with her son in Brittany. By the beginning of October all was ready and she sent word that the revolt would begin on the 18th of that month, then moved to join her husband at Lathom, the Lancashire stronghold of the Stanleys, to await developments. Unhappily for her, the Kentish men, ever-eager to repeat their profitable forays under Wat Tyler and Jack Cade, rose two weeks before the appointed time and, with no support from the west country or from Buckingham's Welshmen, and no sign of Henry Tudor's invasion fleet, the southerners' ardour was quickly quelled by John Howard, Duke of Norfolk.

News of the rising reached King Richard at Lincoln as he neared the end of his grand tour and he immediately summoned supporters to rally to his standard at Leicester by October 22nd, naming Buckingham "false traitor and most untrue creature living" as the leader of the revolt. Henry Stafford had marched from Brecknock on the day appointed by his aunt with a few hundred

152

followers, in an incessant autumnal downpour. The foul weather, the bad news from Kent and the lack of experienced leadership combined to dishearten Buckingham's feeble army and by the time he reached Weobley, the Duke found he was virtually alone. Even his erstwhile prisoner/adviser, John Morton, had fled to the flatlands in his bishopric, where he had a long-established route for escape to Flanders. Buckingham abandoned his hopeless quest and, disguised as a ragged peasant, went to seek sanctuary with an old, retired servitor who now lived near Weobley.

Richard III was moving towards Buckingham's route when his scouts returned and told of the disappearance of the Welsh forces back to their home territories. His army turned towards the southwest and former Lancastrians and Woodville supporters either fled or came to make their submission. The revolt had fizzled out and Buckingham, betrayed by his old serving-man, was publicly executed in Salisbury market square on November 2nd. Henry Tudor's fleet, reduced by a winter storm to only two vessels, approached Plymouth shortly after Buckingham's demise and realising their case was hopeless, turned tail back to France. Margaret Beaufort's grand design was ruined in less than a month. The King she had planned to destroy was set more firmly on his throne than ever and, worst of all, her part in the planning of the revolt was known to him. Retribution must now surely follow and the First Lady of Lancaster would be lucky indeed to keep her head.

In the event Richard, failing to realise that Lord Stanley had been privy to the planning of the abortive rebellion, was content that Lady Margaret's name should not be included amongst those attainted of treason by the Parliament of 1484. However, she had to forfeit all her titles and estates, plus the income granted under her pre-marriage contract with Thomas Stanley, and her right to inherit the lands left by her mother was also cancelled. All her properties were granted to Stanley, who was instructed to keep his wife confined in some secret place, without the servants from her own household, an order which was honoured more in the breach. Margaret Beaufort was able to maintain her correspondence with her son and with John Morton, and, through her husband's ever-increasing influence in State affairs, continued to find means of furthering the Beaufort cause, which had now become inseparable from that of Henry Tudor.

Henry VII

(Detail from the w.w.w.)

Towards the end of July 1485, news came to Margaret Beaufort at her residence in Deeping, that her son's expedition would set sail from Harfleur on the first day of August. With him he would bring John de Vere, and his uncle Jasper Tudor, formerly Earls of Oxford and Pembroke respectively, sundry gentlemen who had fled England following the unsuccessful rising two years previously and some 2,000 men-at-arms who were largely the products of the French penal system and, therefore, of uncertain quality as fighting men. Not an impressive train for a would-be king, but all those concerned knew this would be their last throw of the dice in the great game they were playing. French patience with their non-paying guest was growing short and it was likely that future demands from King Richard for Tudor to be surrendered to his justice might well meet with a more amenable response than had formerly been the case.

The Lady Margaret started to play her own allotted part in the impending drama immediately. Over the past two years of enforced idleness, she had maintained secret links with supporters of Lancaster around the southern counties of England and now alerted them to the impending invasion. Thomas Stanley was in attendance on the King at Nottingham and she sent urgently to him to come to Deeping. When her husband arrived two days later and she told him of the imminent arrival of her son on the Welsh coast, his reaction was not one of unalloyed enthusiasm. He was one of the wealthiest men in England and had no wish to throw away all he had gained through an almost uncanny ability for backing the winning side over the struggle of the past 30 years. His stepson was untried in battle, virtually unknown to the people of the country he aspired to rule and his rag-tag army would make little impression on the war-hardened veterans King Richard would bring down from the Border lands.

Sensing his reluctance, Margaret Beaufort magnified her son's opportunity and his prospects for rapidly increasing his strength once he landed to claim his Kingdom. Wales would rally to his standard, so too the old Lancastrian interest and the rump of the Woodvilles, encouraged by the prospect of the promised match between Henry Tudor and Elizabeth of York, would rise with the rest. Nor could the King count too safely on the northern men; his chief Lieutenant there, Harry Percy of Northumberland, was no leader of warriors and Richard Ratcliffe was continually riding hither and thither on the King's business in other parts. As for London, the capital had always been a law unto itself on the question of loyalty to the country's rulers and the citizens and Aldermen had already noted Richard's preference for northern parts and men. Thomas Stanley must see that now was the time to switch his power yet again to back a new King, whose success would, after all, make him stepfather to a reigning Monarch.

Hesitantly still, Stanley agreed with his wife but insisted that the best strategy would still be to work covertly for Henry's benefit, so that the King was kept in ignorance of his change in allegiance until it was too late for effective counteraction and with this Margaret Beaufort had to be content. Her own case was different in that an invasion by her son must implicate her irretrievably in the supporting treachery and even the mercy of Richard III would be hard-stretched to overlook a second accusation of High Treason. Indeed, it would not be surprising if there were to be thoughts of her arrest when news of Henry's landing came, and these were unlikely to be implemented so long as her husband had the King's confidence. Stanley rode back to Nottingham intent on doing nothing without due thought; there would be a time for action and, when it came, he must strike hard and decisively, in whatever direction might be required, to assure his own safety and future well-being.

Battle-flag of Thomas, second Lord Stanley.

CHAPTER NINETEEN

"For God's sake, let us sit upon the ground,
And tell sad stories of the death of kings."
[Richard II]

To Lady Margaret, waiting anxiously in Deeping, messengers arrived in mid-August to tell of her son's landing at Milford Haven days earlier. He requested, urgently, as much money as she was able to send to him and the weary heralds, after a few hours of rest and freshly mounted, left again for the Welsh border, where they made safe rendezvous with Tudor's army near Shrewsbury. With the funds from his mother, Henry Tudor also received news that a large force under his stepfather's command was camped between Newport and Stafford, while Sir William Stanley sent word that he was moving steadily southwards from Cheshire with another well-armed body of men and would meet the invading army within a few days. Tudor moved quickly forward to Newport in hope of joining with Lord Stanley, but found that nobleman had already moved eastwards. However, Sir Gilbert Talbot, whose family had no love for the House of York, was there with 500 men more to serve under the Welsh Dragon banner.

Reaching Stafford on the 16th of August, Henry Tudor found that his elusive stepfather had moved ahead of him again, this time to Lichfield, but his growing impatience was salved to some extent by a meeting with William Stanley who assured him of the family's support and said that Lord Thomas would leave artillery and supplies for him to collect as he passed through Lichfield. Henry Tudor found the cannon and munitions awaiting his arrival in the town as William Stanley had told him and, better equipped for battle, his army moved on towards Tamworth. There, late in the evening of August 19th, scouts from Thomas Stanley came to the pretender's tent and led him to the village of Atherstone, where he met for the first time with his stepfather and with William Stanley, who had now been proclaimed a traitor by the King and whose life was already forfeit in consequence.

Tudor anxiously demanded that their three armies should unite at once and march together against King Richard, but Lord Stanley had deeper games to play. His son, Lord Strange, was with the King as hostage so an open declaration of support was out of the question. However, Henry Tudor was assured that when his army met that of the King, both Stanleys would be close at hand with considerable force and would join in the fighting on Tudor's side. With this, Margaret Beaufort's son had to be content, and he rode back with the news to John de Vere, erstwhile Earl of Oxford, who commanded his army. Oxford felt that, at worst, the King would be deprived of reinforcement by the Stanleys and, at best, their surprise entry into the battle in support of the rebels could prove a decisive advantage. He proposed, therefore, that they should recommence their march towards Leicester on the following morning, Saturday, August 20th and Henry Tudor gave his grudging assent.

In the late afternoon of August 21st, the Tudor army made camp on open land called White Moors, which lay midway between the villages of Dadlington and Shenton. Here Oxford's scouts returned quickly from their reconnaissance with news that King Richard's army was only two miles to their front at a village called Sutton Cheney. Enemy scouts had also been spotted observing their own army's location and it was clear that an engagement could be expected on the following day. There was still no word from either of the Stanley brothers, who were reported as encamped to north and south of the main opposing armies, but Oxford took comfort from the fact that neither had joined the King's force and settled his army for the night, with advance warning to his commanders that, on the morrow, they would advance to fight what must inevitably be a decisive encounter.

Early the next morning, Oxford led his army forward along their road to Leicester. About a mile along the way, the Sence Brook ran across their route but it was easily fordable at the height of summer and they crossed and continued towards Ambion Hill, a spur of high ground overlooking a redemoor, or flat, marshy plain, at its foot. On the narrow brow of the hill, Oxford could see movement and light glinting off spear points and armour. The point of the high ground was covered with a defensive wall of men-at-arms, towards which the Tudor column was advancing. Just beyond bowshot, Oxford found his horses moving with increasing difficulty through boggy ground, which he knew must cut up badly as more of his men passed through it and required immediate adjustment of his line of advance, if the whole force

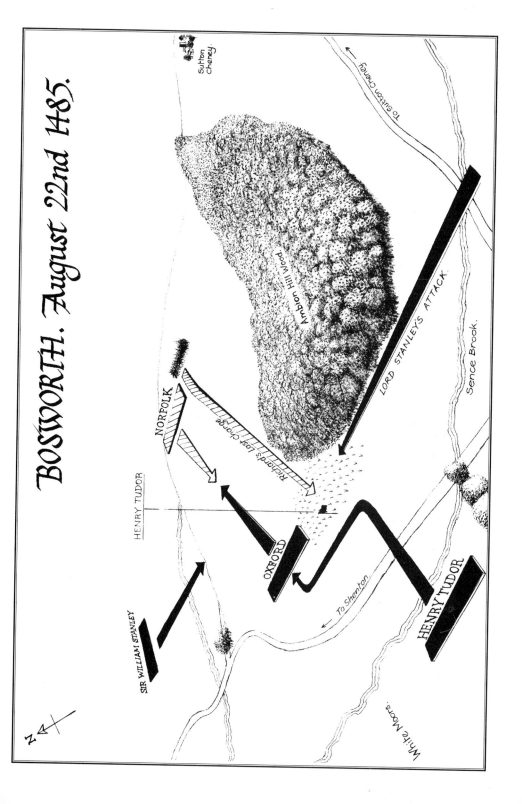

BOSWORTH. August 22nd 1485.

N

To Sutton Cheney.

Sutton Cheney.

Ambion Hill Wood.

Lord Stanley's Attack.

Sence Brook.

Norfolk

Richard's Last Charge.

Henry Tudor

Oxford

To Shenton.

Sir William Stanley

Henry Tudor.

White Moors.

were not to become inextricably mired in the marsh-land.

Looking again at Ambion's brow, he could see only one small body of cavalry on the extreme left flank of the hill, grouped around the royal standard. The rest of the Yorkist line seemed to consist entirely of footmen and artillery, which would make it reasonably safe to wheel his army by their left and form line after marching across the enemy front. This he did, and England's King who, as any experienced General would, had arrayed his army to cover all contingencies, had to watch Tudor's forces manoeuvre freely, some 300 yards below him. This, because his cavalry were held in reserve, watching large bodies of men which had appeared about a mile off to the right and left of his position and, at the same time, keeping an eye on the clearly reluctant support from 2,000 men under Harry Percy who crowded the hill behind the King's main force.

When his whole array was formed, Oxford prepared to make a general advance in line, across and up the hill, leaving only a small section of his rearguard protected by the marsh which had enforced the detour and, in the centre of which, was an unhappy Henry Tudor, dressed in full plate armour, and involved in his first-ever battle. The Yorkist artillery and archers opened on their enemy and Oxford ordered reply in kind, until all ammunition from the supply left by Stanley was used, and then ordered his line to advance up the hill towards the waiting foe, where the banners of John Howard, Duke of Norfolk waved on the right of the Yorkist array. As Oxford's line advanced, Norfolk's men, keen to get to closer quarters, moved down the hill to meet them and the two armies became locked in a fight to the death in the middle of the slope.

King Richard, noting that the two flanking forces led by the Stanleys were drawing ever nearer the scene of the action, continued his strategy of watch and wait before committing his main cavalry, in the hope that Norfolk's men would drive Oxford's line back down the hill. Unfortunately for him, John de Vere was holding his position well and, suddenly, William Stanley, already attainted as a traitor and with nothing to lose, led a charge into Norfolk's right flank. With Norfolk's line starting to buckle and Thomas Stanley continuing to advance on the other flank, Richard decided on immediate action and, sending to his reserves to follow him and his personal guard, he charged down the slope towards the small group of mounted men centred on the Tudor banner. Thus did the King add one last, fatal blunder to

**Traditional portrait of Thomas, Second Lord Stanley,
later Earl of Derby, Step-father of Henry Tudor.**

the catalogue of tactical errors, which had led him to Ambion Hill and would end in his death.

The initial impact of the King's charge drove through the line protecting Henry Tudor and William Brandon, proud bearer of Cadwallader's banner, was cut down by Richard himself. The giant Sir John Cheyney interposed his armoured body between the charging axe and the shrinking Tudor and was knocked down for his pains. Success, it seemed, was but a few strides forward, when the King's great charger, unable to keep a firm footing on the marshy ground, slipped and fell. Thomas Stanley, by now close to the scene and ready to commit his men to whichever side had the upper hand, saw the royal helmet fall and assumed that Richard had been slain. Waving his sword and shouting loudly for Tudor, he led his men at the gallop towards the group surrounding the body of his late liege-lord and then, to his horror, saw the King was on his feet and shouting for a remount on which to lead a final, mortal charge at the pretender. Lord Thomas Stanley, for the first time in his life, found himself committed to the wrong side at the critical point in a struggle and took the only option left to him. He and his force charged down on the King and his few remaining guards and ended the life of the last of the Plantagenets. Richard's last words as he died were "Treason, Treason…"

The Wars of the Roses – as they were never called during the thirty years they lasted – were over. The House of Plantagenet, which had ruled England and much of France for three centuries, was extinguished, brought to final ruin by the bastard sprig, which had sprung from its loins. Henry Tudor, half-Beaufort, half-Franco/Welsh commoner, graciously accepted the crown of England, on the field of his greatest victory, earned for him by the fighting courage of John de Vere and the treachery of his mother's kindred. Now he would mete out swift justice to those who had opposed his right of succession and think of suitable reward for any who had helped him to the throne. But first, he must send news of his triumph to his dear mother, the last of the Beauforts, whose pride in her descent, so typical of all her line, had helped her to overcome, finally, the humiliation of the royal bar sinister. That unacceptable stigma, which for far too long had kept the kingly stock of John of Gaunt from their rightful place on England's throne.

Epilogue

"Kings"

Effigy of Margaret Beaufort

(Detail from the w.w.w.)

Margaret Beaufort, last of her line, never ceased to work for the aggrandisement of her son, first of the House of Tudor to wear a royal crown.

All her titles and lands were restored to her in Henry's first Parliament and, in addition, her devoted son presented her with a magnificent London residence, Coldharbour, which overlooked the Thames. Here she would, additionally, oversee the training of Elizabeth of York, as Henry's bride-to-be prepared for her future role as Queen of England. Here also, she would guard Edward, Earl of Warwick and son of George of Clarence, potential chief pretender to her son's throne, and Edward Stafford, third Duke of Buckingham, another possible claimant whose wardship was undoubtedly the most profitable of all the English nobility. Only the mother of the King was, like Caesar's wife, above suspicion in the eyes of her ever-distrustful son.

The Lady Margaret, now Countess of Derby in light of her husband's elevation to the royal title, dedicated the rest of her life to sharing her son's burden of kingship, to the management of her own vast estates, and to good works and prayers. To allow her time and space to manage all these affairs, she, with the agreement of her husband, assumed the status of "femme seule", formally taking vows of chastity when aged 56. She made her confession at least twice a week, took only one meal a day during Lent, and maintained 12 paupers in the almshouse attached to her manor at Collyweston, supervising their care personally, when they were sick or near death. She was at her prie-dieu so regularly, and for prayers so protracted, as to damage her back thus making her regular oblations still more painful.

A year after taking her vows, she was saddened by news of the death of her friend and co-conspirator of many years, John Morton, who had risen, thanks to the progressive benefactions of the King he had helped to create, to be named as Cardinal-Archbishop of Canterbury and Chancellor of England. Morton, having himself become a man of great wealth, left Lady Margaret "a portraiture of Our Lady in pure gold", as a mark of his esteem. Three years on, the King's mother lost another faithful servant in Sir Reginald Bray KG, who had borne her secret messages to Henry Tudor in France and to John Morton in Brecknock and had become a notably hard collector of the latter's tax exactions on behalf of his new master. In his will Bray noted that all his wealth, and everything he had achieved in his life, was due to that great lady, Margaret Beaufort. A year later still, Thomas Stanley, Earl of Derby, went to meet his final judgement, but whether his widow offered prayers for his soul is not recorded. However, she was largely responsible for the installation of his second son, James, in the Bishopric of Ely, once Morton's See, where the younger Stanley impressed only by his worldliness and lack of learning.

The natural cycle of death, of all those who had played some part in the shaping of her life, was made complete when her beloved son died at his palace of Richmond on the 21st day of April 1509, aged 52. Henry Tudor had ruled England for short of 24 years and amassed a fortune in treasure alone, equivalent to three and a quarter billion pounds in twenty first century terms. He also left a single son, who was more Plantagenet than Tudor, ran through his patrimony in short space, destroyed the church to which his father and grandmother had been devoted in order to replenish his coffers, and to permit him licence to become England's most-married king. Margaret Beaufort, perhaps with some inexplicable foreknowledge of what was to come, is said to have wept profusely on the occasion of the coronation of Henry VIII, a ceremony she was too enfeebled to attend.

Then, having executed her son's last Will and testament, instructed her eighteen year old grandson as to whom he should select for his Council and concerning his marriage to Catherine of Aragon, the last of the Beauforts retired from involvement in affairs of state to await her own assignation with the last debt-collector. She died some ten weeks after her son, on June 29, 1509, reportedly after dining on a cygnet. John Fisher, Lady Margaret's chaplain and confessor during the last seven years of her life and a famous sermoniser, said in his memorial address a month after her death that she had a difficult end, crying out at the pain.

It may be that all the trumpets sounded on the other side for the passing of the last of the Beaufort Pride. Or, perhaps they did not.

Signature of Henry VII

(G. Wheeler)

ACKNOWLEDGEMENTS

Consistent with my long-established policy of always saying please and thank you, I received invaluable help in sourcing information for this book from my friend and fellow Ricardian, Christine Symonds, whom the Yorkshire Branch of the Society is privileged to have as its Librarian and for this, and similar help with every work I have produced, thank you Christine.

Similarly, I am bound to record my gratitude to Geoffrey Wheeler, custodian of the Richard III Society's photographic archives, whose contribution to this book is appropriately marked in the relevant pages. Further help with illustrations came from my friend and fellow Ricardian, Ralph Taylor, whose pencil portraits of three of the principal characters have added a totally new dimension to my work.

Yet another Ricardian has played her usual key role in producing my book, Pam Benstead of our Worcester Branch, who wrote mild criticism of an early work and was immediately co-opted to prevent similar failings in any future writings. She and her husband Bill have become dear friends during the past five years and I am delighted that producing this book enables me to express again my sincere gratitude for her long-suffering forbearance with my punctuational peccadilloes.

And to dear Maureen Bush, Curator of Middleham Castle, without whose encouragement and support all my efforts could well have been vain, my eternal gratitude.

Finally, I would like to thank the husband and wife team who have produced all my books, Allan and Kath Holdsworth, who, with their dedicated team at Pennine Printing Services Ltd., could not have been more helpful through the years. And another thanks to my first helper and friend in the book-writing field, Roy Barton, who drew the original battlemaps for "Hollow Crowns" which I have used repeatedly through the series.

What a wonderful "second-career" all of you launched me upon. What wonderful friends you have been.

SOURCES

The most important general sources of material for "A Pride of Bastards" were:

The Fifteenth Century by E.F. Jacob, sometime Chichele Professor of Modern History in Oxford University.

History of England by Sir Charles Oman.

Genesis of Lancaster, Volume 2, by Sir James Ramsay.

The Fourteenth Century by May McKisack, sometime Professor of History at Westfield College, University of London.

Of particular value to me, however, in grasping fundamental truths about the period were two books:

The Agincourt War by Alfred H. Burne, undoubtedly, with its companion volume The Crecy War, the most authoritative work on the Hundred Years War

A History of the Manor and Rectory of Kettlethorpe by R.E.G. Cole MA, Prebendary of Lincoln. This little pamphlet reveals more than the good churchman perhaps intended to say about Katherine Swynford and John of Gaunt, and their relationship, and this writer found it infinitely more enlightening than Anya Seton, (who used it as the basis for her romantic factional work, "Katherine",) appears to have done.

Other regularly consulted authorities on the period included Black's English History, Warkworth, Bentley, and the perennial Kendall's "Richard III".

All the above repay additional reading. The only other major source unfortunately does not, since it is my own voluminous notes, largely illegible except to me and my quondam secretary and shortly to be consigned to that great filing cabinet in the sky. It is finished.

Index

170

171

Also available from Baildon Books

Geoffrey Richardson's

THE HOLLOW CROWNS

For the first time – all major battles of the Wars of the Roses
in detail and in one volume.

From the fields and gardens by St Albans on an early Summer's day in 1455, to the death of the last Plantagenet King of England, alone, betrayed and hopelessly mired in marshland below Bosworth's Ambien Hill, the reader is swept along through three decades of English History.

Encountering along the way: the hapless Henry VI, pathetic son of the victor of Agincourt; Margaret of Anjou, Henry's Queen and Lancaster's champion for 20 years; Richard Neville, fabled Kingmaker Warwick, who – the story shows – has enjoyed a greater reputation in history than his deeds warranted; the giant Edward IV, England's greatest Warrior-King, and Richard, his youngest brother, arguably the last true monarch of England and almost certainly the worst-slandered.

This all-new account of the bloodiest 30 years in English History has been termed: "History made easy - and interesting!" Written in a fresh narrative style, with full-page, "3D" Battlemaps of all eleven major conflicts and portraits of the principal participants (including line-drawings of Warwick and Margaret of Anjou developed from computer-enhanced sources) THE HOLLOW CROWNS" puts the story back into History.

ISBN 0 9527621 0 2

AND...

Geoffrey Richardson's

"THE DECEIVERS"

This History covers the last two years of the internecine struggle between York and Lancaster - the so-called Wars of the Roses - from the death of Edward IV in April 1483, to the defeat and death of his successor, Richard III, at Bosworth, and through the early years of the usurper, Henry Tudor, to the end of the 15th Century.

Written in this author's easy narrative style, "The Deceivers" sets out to answer four main questions :

- *Why was the life of William, Lord Hastings ended so abruptly and ingloriously by his former comrade-in-arms -*

- *Why should Henry Stafford, second Duke of Buckingham, rebel against the King he had helped to his throne three months earlier -*

- *How could a seasoned warrior like Richard III lose the Battle of Bosworth against what was, at best, a "rabble in arms" -*

and, most important of all,

- *Who killed the Princes in the Tower, and When, and Why -*

The answers to all these questions are set down in "The Deceivers" and reveal a stunning conspiracy on the part of a handful of people, who have never previously been indicted for the crimes of which they are guilty, but who changed the course of English History.

ISBN 09527621 1 0